Social Issues
in Literature

Gender in Lorraine Hansberry's *A Raisin in the Sun*

Other Books in the Social Issues in Literature Series:

Social Issues in Literature

Gender in Lorraine Hansberry's *A Raisin in the Sun*

Gary Wiener, Book Editor

GREENHAVEN PRESS
A part of Gale, Cengage Learning

GALE
CENGAGE Learning

Detroit • New York • San Francisco • New Haven, Conn • Waterville, Maine • London

Christine Nasso, *Publisher*
Elizabeth Des Chenes, *Managing Editor*

© 2011 Greenhaven Press, a part of Gale, Cengage Learning

Gale and Greenhaven Press are registered trademarks used herein under license.

For more information, contact:
Greenhaven Press
27500 Drake Rd.
Farmington Hills, MI 48331-3535
Or you can visit our Internet site at gale.cengage.com

For product information and technology assistance, contact us at

Gale Customer Support, 1-800-877-4253
For permission to use material from this text or product, submit all requests online at
www.cengage.com/permissions

Further permissions questions can be emailed to permissionrequest@cengage.com

Articles in Greenhaven Press anthologies are often edited for length to meet page requirements. In addition, original titles of these works are changed to clearly present the main thesis and to explicitly indicate the author's opinion. Every effort is made to ensure that Greenhaven Press accurately reflects the original intent of the authors. Every effort has been made to trace the owners of copyrighted material.

Cover image © Bettmann/Corbis.

LIBRARY OF CONGRESS CATALOGING-IN-PUBLICATION DATA

Gender in Lorraine Hansberry's A raisin in the sun / Gary Wiener, book editor.
     p. cm. -- (Social issues in literature)
   Includes bibliographical references and index.
   ISBN 978-0-7377-5022-5 -- ISBN 978-0-7377-5023-2 (pbk.)
   1. Hansberry, Lorraine, 1930-1965. Raisin in the sun--Juvenile literature. 2. Hansberry, Lorraine, 1930-1965--Social and political views--Juvenile literature. 3. African Americans in literature--Juvenile literature. 4. African American families in literature--Juvenile literature. 5. Sex role in literature--Juvenile literature. 6. Sex differences (Psychology)--Juvenile literature. I. Wiener, Gary.
   PS3515.A515R336 2011
   812'.54--dc22
                                                          2010039549

Printed in the United States of America
  2 3 4 5 6   22 21 20 19 18

Contents

As gay African American author Richard Wright does in his works, Hansberry depicts the struggle of Walter, an emasculated male, in *A Raisin in the Sun*. Her solution to Walter's dilemma, however, is artificial and unconvincing.

Chapter 3: Contemporary Perspectives on Gender

Introduction

Male and female gender roles have long been recognized as an important concern in Lorraine Hansberry's *A Raisin in the Sun*. Deemed early on as a play that realistically portrayed an African American family's strengths as well as its dysfunctions, *Raisin* captured the imagination of both white and black audiences through its well-drawn, complex characterizations of Walter, Beneatha, Ruth, and Lena Younger. Where early audiences primarily viewed *Raisin* as a play about race, Hansberry famously attested that it was not a "negro play." This surprised many people and disappointed some, but with that remark Hansberry was pointing out that while any discussion of *Raisin* certainly could not be divorced from the racial implications of its plot and characters, the play was about much more than the color of its protagonists' skin. Always the global thinker, Hansberry was not merely presenting her audience with an attack on racial prejudice—additionally, *A Raisin in the Sun* is a brick thrown through the window of all bigotry and narrow-minded thinking—racism, sexism, religious intolerance, and, even though less overtly, homophobia.

Central to the play's message is the way in which Hansberry complicates traditional gender roles in the Younger family, particularly with regard to its women. Walter, his mother Lena, his sister Beneatha, and his wife, Ruth, all envision ways to improve their lot in life, but their dreams are often at odds not just with white society's plans for African Americans, but with each other's. The imposing matriarch, Lena, makes decisions about spending the large inheritance from her husband without consulting her son; Beneatha dreams of becoming a doctor, a lofty goal for an African American woman in the conservative 1950s, yet she is also, in Bernadette Waterman Ward's words, "an unrealistic, frivolous egotist";[1] and Ruth, pregnant with Walter's second child, investigates abortion, again without consulting the male putative head of the family, her husband Walter. These family dynamics, rooted in gender wars, racial strife, and dreams deferred, drive the play toward its ambiguously happy ending.

But below the surface of Hansberry's drama was her own struggle with gender, which has only come to light in recent years. It is now beyond debate that Hansberry—who married fellow radical protester Robert Nemiroff in 1953, separated from him in 1957, and officially divorced him in 1964—was a closeted gay woman; moreover, at the same time as she was writing *Raisin*, a part of her intellectual energy was given over to the struggle of gays, and more specifically lesbians, in heterosexual America. The 1950s were a particularly socially repressive time. Senator Joseph McCarthy was hunting down anyone with radically liberal or Communist affiliations. Many in the psychiatric community and beyond regarded homosexuality as a mental illness, and the so-called "Lavender Scare" that paralleled McCarthy's "Red Scare" referred to the persecution of gays during that time period. As a secretly gay woman, Lorraine Hansberry was acutely aware of this persecution, and thus, many scholars suggest, the idea of gender in *Raisin* must be broadened to consider alternative sexualities, for this topic was certainly on the mind of its author while she was writing the play.

The substantiation of such assertions surfaced in letters that Hansberry wrote in the 1950s to a lesbian journal, *The Ladder*, run by the San Francisco–based organization the Daughters of Bilitis. These letters were written as she was otherwise busy composing the play that would catapult her to fame. It is an easy leap, therefore, to read in Hansberry's critique of racism and sexism in *A Raisin in the Sun* a subtext that attacks not just these, but all prejudices, including homophobia. But none of this information—about her lesbianism, or even her divorce from Nemiroff—was public information while she was alive. It was only years after her death that scholars began to tie her feminism to her gay identity.

One such scholar, Lisbeth Lipari, sees parallels between Hansberry's views on lesbianism and her attitude toward race in *A Raisin in the Sun*: "Hansberry's critique of separatism in [her] letter [to the *Ladder*] also resonates with her rejection of the kind of racial separatism advocated by black nationalism as expressed in her plays," Lipari writes.[2] In her letters to the lesbian magazine, Hansberry had argued against fostering "strict separatist notions, homo or hetero." This desire to find a way to express one's identity within society coincides, Lipari writes, with Hansberry's stance against the black Muslims and other groups who advocated a separatist agenda. In *Raisin*, Beneatha argues eloquently that black independence essentially solves nothing, and that racism must be dealt with from within the larger society and not from without.

Whatever the source of Hansberry's feminism, whether derived simply from her understanding of women as less privileged than their male counterparts or driven by her clandestine gay identity, Hansberry's writings anticipate the women's liberation movement that came to the forefront in America shortly after her death. As Hansberry observed in an interview with the well-known social historian Studs Terkel in 1959, "Obviously the most oppressed group of any oppressed group will be its women, who are twice oppressed."[3] This double oppression is dramatized in *Raisin*'s women: Mama, who has lost her husband, attempts to keep her family together even as she works long hours as a domestic for a wealthy white family; Beneatha endures the sexism of her conservative middle-class boyfriend, her African mentor and would-be lover, and her selfish brother; and Ruth takes in laundry from white families and seeks a way to terminate part of her family's future through abortion. These long-suffering, headstrong women are simultaneously resilient and fragile, summing up all of the dualities associated with being a female in the traditionalist

1950s. But Hansberry always had an eye for the larger picture. According to Steven R. Carter, "It was also important, in her view, for women to perceive the connection between their oppression (along with that of race, class, and ethnicity) and that of other groups, such as homosexuals, and the dangerous effects of ignoring such connections."[4] As feminist author bell hooks writes, "Hansberry linked feminism and gay rights long before it was popular to do so."[5]

So, even in their triumphant moment at the end of the play, when Mama's decision to move to the all-white Clybourne Park in the face of neighborhood opposition finds universal support in the Younger family, when Walter proudly informs neighborhood spokesman Karl Lindner that Beneatha is going to be a doctor, when Beneatha decides to move to Africa with Joseph Asagai, and when Ruth decides to keep her baby and work (even if she has to strap it to her back while doing so), there is ambiguity and potential trouble looming ahead. Witness Lindner's ominous warning: "I hope you people know what you're in for." Nevertheless, as bell hooks writes of Hansberry, "All her writing is deeply optimistic. Her work is hopeful, yet that hope is never based on false sentimentality. It is always rooted in activism."[6] Hansberry herself would never live to see the fulfillment of her vision of social justice that would begin with the civil rights movement, the women's liberation movement, and the Stonewall riot of 1969 that ushered in the gay rights movement. Prescient as she was, moving the Youngers into that all-white neighborhood in the late 1950s would be, she knew, fraught with all of the turbulent drama of those times that she never lived to see.

The selections in *Social Issues in Literature: Gender in Lorraine Hansberry's "A Raisin in the Sun"* survey the many gender issues that Hansberry dramatizes in her play. They demonstrate how she was ahead of her time in her attitudes toward masculinity and femininity. They investigate how, as hooks writes, "Looking at the world from a standpoint that recognized the interconnectedness of race, sex, and class, she challenged everyone who encountered her work."[7] These selections examine how she undermined, reinterpreted, and transformed traditional male-female roles in her exploration of gender in post–World War II America. Finally, the selections in the last chapter explore the complexity of gender issues in contemporary society.

Notes

1. Bernadette Waterman Ward, "Silencing Lorraine Hansberry" in *Life and Learning X*. Conference Proceedings of University Faculty for Life, 2002, pp. 339. Reprinted in *Pro-Life Feminism: Yesterday and Today*, eds. Rachel McNair, Mary Krane Derr, and Linda Naranjo-Huebl. Kansas City, MO: Feminism and Nonviolence Studies Association, 2005.

2. Lisbeth Lipari, "The Rhetoric of Intersectionality: Lorraine Hansberry's 1957 Letters to the *Ladder*," in *Queering Public Address: Sexualities in American Historical Discourse*, ed. Charles E. Morris. Studies in Rhetoric/Communication. Columbia: University of South Carolina Press, 2007, p. 230.

3. Lorraine Hansberry, "Make New Sounds: Studs Terkel Interviews Lorraine Hansberry," *American Theatre*, November 1984, p. 6.

4. Steven R. Carter, *Hansberry's Drama: Commitment amid Complexity*. Urbana: University of Illinois Press, 1991, p. 5.

5. bell hooks, *Remembered Rapture: The Writer at Work*. New York: Henry Holt, 1999, p. 218.

6. hooks, *Remembered Rapture*, p. 218.

7. hooks, *Remembered Rapture*, pp. 218–219.

Chronology

1930

Lorraine Vivian Hansberry is born in Chicago, Illinois, on May 19.

1938

Hanberry's family moves into a white neighborhood; residents protest and throw a brick through the window; the family loses a lawsuit challenging segregated housing.

1940

The U.S. Supreme Court finds in favor of the Hansberrys in the case *Hansberry v. Lee*; Hansberry's father, Carl, runs for Congress and loses.

1944

Hansberry enters Englewood High School and wins a writing award during her freshman year.

1946

Carl Hansberry dies in Mexico.

1947

Hansberry is elected president of her high school debating society.

1948

Hansberry graduates from Englewood High School. She enters the University of Wisconsin. She sees the Irish play *Juno and the Paycock*, which influences her greatly.

1949

Hansberry studies art at the University of Guadalajara in Mexico.

1950

Hansberry drops out of the University of Wisconsin and moves to New York City.

1951

Hansberry joins the staff of Paul Robeson's publication *Freedom*.

1952

Hansberry meets Robert Nemiroff at a protest in New York City.

1953

Hansberry and Nemiroff marry and live in Greenwich Village; she resigns from *Freedom* to pursue playwriting.

1957

She finishes writing *A Raisin in the Sun*.

1959

A Raisin in the Sun, starring Sidney Poitier, debuts on Broadway; the play wins the New York Drama Critics' Circle Award.

1960

Hansberry writes the screenplay for the film version of *A Raisin in the Sun*.

1961

The film version of *A Raisin in the Sun*, starring Sidney Poitier, is released and wins an award at the Cannes Film Festival.

1963

Hansberry falls ill and is diagnosed with cancer.

1964

Hansberry and Nemiroff divorce on March 10. Her second play, *The Sign in Sidney Brustein's Window*, opens.

1965

Hansberry dies on January 12. *The Sign in Sidney Brustein's Window* closes the same day.

1967

Nemiroff produces *Lorraine Hansberry in Her Own Words*, a radio documentary.

1969

To Be Young Gifted and Black, Hansberry's autobiography, is published; a play based on her autobiography opens off-Broadway.

1970

Hansberry's unfinished play, *Les Blancs*, completed by Nemiroff, opens on Broadway.

1973

Nemiroff produces a musical version of *A Raisin in the Sun*, titled *Raisin*, which wins a Tony Award for best Broadway musical.

1989

The twentieth anniversary of *A Raisin in the Sun* is marked by revivals, including a new television version starring Danny Glover and Esther Rolle.

1991

Robert Nemiroff dies.

2004

A revival of *A Raisin in the Sun*, starring rapper/entrepreneur Sean "P. Diddy" Combs, opens on Broadway. The premiere is attended by Oprah Winfrey, Spike Lee, Beyoncé Knowles, and Jay Z, among others. Audra McDonald (as Ruth) and Phylicia Rashad (as Lena) win Tony Awards.

2008

A new television version of *A Raisin in the Sun*, also starring Sean Combs, is produced.

Social Issues in Literature

CHAPTER 1

Background on Lorraine Hansberry

The Life of Lorraine Hansberry

Contemporary Heroes and Heroines

Contemporary Heroes and Heroines is a Gale Research reference work for young people, containing biographical profiles of exemplary people.

The following selection explains how Lorraine Hansberry grew up in the Chicago area, the daughter of upwardly mobile African American parents. The central event of her young life occurred when her family moved into a white neighborhood in the suburbs and an angry mob gathered outside of the house. This storyline was fictionalized in A Raisin in the Sun. As an adult, Hansberry was a tireless activist for social justice, becoming famous and controversial enough to warrant surveillance by the FBI. Hansberry's early death from cancer cut short the career of not only a promising writer but also a devoted spokesperson for the downtrodden in America.

Born May 19, 1930, in Chicago, Illinois, Lorraine Hansberry was the first American dramatist to create a realistic portrayal of an urban, working-class African American family. She was also an outspoken political and social activist. She died on January 12, 1965, in New York, New York.

With the debut of her 1959 drama *A Raisin in the Sun*—the first play by an African American woman ever to run on Broadway—Lorraine Hansberry ushered in a new era of United States theater history. "I had never in my life seen so many black people in the theater," fellow writer James Baldwin later noted in the introduction to Hansberry's autobiography.

Contemporary Heroes and Heroines, Book III, "Lorraine Hansberry," edited by Terrie M. Rooney, Detroit, MI: Gale, 1998. Copyright © 1998 by Gale. Reproduced by permission of Gale, a part of Cengage Learning.

"And the reason was that never before, in the entire history of the American theater, had so much of the truth of black people's lives been seen on the stage." *A Raisin in the Sun* went on to win the New York Drama Critics Circle Award for best play of the year. Hansberry thus became the first African American writer, the fifth woman, and the youngest American playwright ever to receive the honor.

But Hansberry did more than just expand the content of realistic stage drama to include African Americans. She was also a political and social activist whose concerns ranged from racism and homophobia to Pan-Africanism [a movement to unite those of African descent], McCarthyism[1] , and global issues of war and peace. Her links to such groups as the Student Nonviolent Coordinating Committee (SNCC), the Communist party, and various black nationalist groups made her the target of U.S. government surveillance, as did her outspokenness. But only death was finally able to silence the woman who had so aptly defined what it meant "to be young, gifted and black."

Youth in Chicago

A native of Chicago, Hansberry was the youngest of four children. She grew up in a comfortable, upper-middle-class African American neighborhood on the city's South Side. Her parents, Carl Augustus and Nannie (Perry) Hansberry, had done quite well financially after Carl gave up his job as a bank teller to become an entrepreneur. His innovative, small-scale "kitchenette" for one- or two-bedroom apartments brought him success in real estate during the Great Depression. Carl tried his hand at politics, too, campaigning door-to-door throughout his neighborhood in 1940 in what turned out to be an unsuccessful bid for a seat in the U.S. Congress.

1. Named for Joseph McCarthy, a U.S. senator from Wisconsin in the 1950s, McCarthyism involved widespread accusations of Communist affiliations, disloyalty, and treason issued against prominent people in government, business, and the arts without proper evidence.

Hansberry's extended family was also well known in the African American community both at a local and a national level for their commitment to the fight for black liberation. In fact, her parents turned their home into a social center for distinguished African American intellectuals and artists. Visitors included noted sociologist W.E.B. Du Bois and singer Paul Robeson, both of whom would later play more significant formative roles in Hansberry's life. And Hansberry's mother ensured that her children were in touch with their roots by taking them to visit their grandmother in Tennessee, where they heard stories of how their enslaved grandfather had run away and hidden from his master in the very same hills they could see from the homestead.

But the event that probably left the strongest impression on young Hansberry—an event that she later incorporated into her most famous play—occurred in 1938, when her parents decided to move from the South Side and buy a larger home that happened to be located in a predominantly white neighborhood. While sitting on the porch of their new house one day, eight-year-old Lorraine and her sister, Mamie, watched an angry white mob gather out front. Frightened, the girls retreated into the living room. Then a brick suddenly came crashing through the front window (narrowly missing Lorraine) and lodged itself in the opposite wall.

Writing in the biography *Lorraine Hansberry*, Anne Cheney quoted Hansberry's ex-husband, Robert Nemiroff, on the effect the episode had had on his former wife. Observed Nemiroff: "Who knows which part had the greatest impact on the child—the brick? The mother sitting up nights with a gun? The incidents to and from school? The father away in Washington? The fact that the cops did not defend the home but that blacks had to come from outside to do so? The fact that the family was then evicted by the Supreme Court of Illinois?" The case went all the way to the U.S. Supreme Court in a test of Chicago's restrictive real estate covenants. In a historic 1940 decision, Carl Hansberry won. Thus, his daughter grew up firmly believing in the value of challenging the status quo, no matter what sacrifices were necessary.

College in Wisconsin

In 1948, after graduating from high school, Hansberry headed off to the University of Wisconsin. Forced to live off campus because there was no on-campus housing available for African American students, she commuted each day to attend classes in literature, history, philosophy, art, mathematics, and science. Excited by her humanities classes and bored by the sciences, Hansberry barely maintained the minimum grade-point average she needed to be allowed to stay in school.

Outside of class, she developed a variety of interests. A production of Irish playwright Sean O'Casey's *Juno and the Paycock* gave flight to her imagination and prompted her to study the works of modern masters such as Henrik Ibsen and August Strindberg. It also inspired her to participate in student theater productions. At the same time, Hansberry found herself increasingly drawn to political activism. During the fall term of her second year, for example, she became campus chair of the Young Progressives of America in support of Henry Wallace's 1948 presidential bid. His defeat left her disillusioned with party politics. But Hansberry continued to enjoy her friendships with visiting African students and a number of young campus radicals. Many of them later appeared as characters in a section of her unfinished autobiographical novel *All the Dark and Beautiful Warriors*.

As fulfilling as Hansberry's off-campus activities might have been, however, a variety of social and racial obstacles stood in the path of her academic success at the University of Wisconsin. In a theater class on set design during her second year, for instance, she received a D from a professor who considered her work above average but who said he did not want to encourage a young black woman to enter a white-dominated field. Dissatisfied with her classes and dismayed by such attitudes, Hansberry left Wisconsin in 1950 and headed for New York City.

Life in New York City

There, the fledgling writer enrolled at the New School for Social Research, wrote articles for a publication of the Young Progressives of America, and, in 1951, joined the staff of Paul Robeson's magazine *Freedom*. Over the next three years, Hansberry traveled extensively on assignment for *Freedom*, covering the United States, Africa, and South America. Among the articles she wrote were pieces on women, social issues in New York, and the arts. And as her writing skills improved, her politics became more radical. "Shuttling about the city—from the Waldorf-Astoria [Hotel] to Broadway back to Harlem schools—Lorraine Hansberry *did* sharpen her journalistic tools," observed Cheney. "She learned to interview easily; she started to sift important figures from mazes of paper; she began to penetrate the facades of people and events." By the time Hansberry was in her mid-twenties, she had made up her mind to combine a life of activism with her desire to write for the stage.

Hansberry also developed her public speaking skills by teaching classes at Frederick Douglass School in Harlem and by attending and speaking at political rallies. It was at a 1951 rally protesting the exclusion of African American players from the basketball team at New York University (NYU) that Hansberry met Robert Nemiroff, a Jewish graduate student in literature at the university. Hansberry worked for a while in the Greenwich Village restaurant owned by Nemiroff's family. The two young activists developed a close relationship, and on June 20, 1953, they were married.

During the next few years Hansberry worked at a variety of jobs, including that of a typist, secretary, recreation leader

Lorraine Hansberry. AP Images.

for the Federation for the Handicapped, and occasional con-
tributor to *Freedom* before it went bankrupt in 1955. Nemiroff, meanwhile, had graduated with his master's degree
from NYU and become first a reader and copywriter for Sears

Readers' Club and then promotions director of Avon Books. Together they reveled in the rich cultural milieu of Greenwich Village, marched on picket lines, attended all-night vigils for desegregation, and enjoyed the company of friends. Hansberry would later write about these times in her play *The Sign in Sidney Brustein's Window*.

A Raisin in the Sun and Fame

In 1956, Robert Nemiroff and a friend, Burt D'ugoff, wrote a song together for which Hansberry suggested the title, "Cindy, Oh, Cindy." It became a hit, and the income they earned from it freed both Hansberry and Nemiroff to write full time. It was then that she began working on what would become *A Raisin in the Sun*, an acknowledged classic of the American theater that blends personal experience with penetrating social criticism.

In *A Raisin in the Sun*, Hansberry depicts a set of events with which she was all too familiar. The story centers on the tribulations of the Youngers, an African American, working-class family living in a cramped apartment on Chicago's South Side during the 1950s. They want nothing more than to claim their share of the "American Dream" and its promise of a comfortable and prosperous life. But when they try to buy a house in an upper-class, white suburb, they find themselves caught up in the racial tensions of the era. A man from the "improvement association" in their new neighborhood offers them money to keep them from moving in and suggests that some family members might meet with violence if they follow through with their plans. But the Youngers refuse to give up on their dream, and as the play ends, they prepare to meet the challenges ahead of them with dignity and determination.

Theater critics and audiences alike—black as well as white—responded to the realism and drama in *A Raisin in the Sun* with tremendous enthusiasm. Hansberry became famous virtually overnight; two years later, she enjoyed another round of success upon the release of the film version of the play, which she herself had adapted for the screen.

With the fame Hansberry enjoyed as a celebrated playwright came numerous chances to act on her political views. She supported a variety of causes that were very unpopular at the time, and she also had close ties to groups some people considered dangerous to the United States government— groups such as the Student Nonviolent Coordinating Committee (SNCC), the Communist party, and various black nationalist organizations. As a result, she came under the surveillance of the Federal Bureau of Investigation (FBI).

Continued Playwriting and Activism

Yet in print and at the podium, Hansberry did not hesitate to continue to speak out on issues of importance to her. In a 1962 speech delivered at a rally calling for the abolishment of the House Un-American Activities Committee (HUAC) [which led anti-Communist investigations], for example, she reflected on the role of the artist in the struggle for justice and freedom. Noted Hansberry: "One can become detached in this world of ours; we can get to a place where we read only the theatre or photography or music pages of our newspapers. And then we wake up one day and find that the better people of our nation are still where they were when we last noted them: in the courts defending *our* constitutional rights for us. . . . I think that all of us who are thinking about such things, who wish to exercise these rights . . . , must really exercise them. Speaking to my fellow artists in particular, I think that we must paint them, sing them, write about them."

In addition to her political activism, Hansberry also found time to do more writing. As early as 1959, she had begun doing the research for a second play, *The Sign in Sidney Brustein's Window*, which was produced in 1964. The story of a Jewish intellectual who wavers between being politically committed and totally disillusioned, it was not a success critically or commercially and closed after only 101 performances. Hansberry wrote several other plays (published and unpublished), including *The Arrival of Mr. Todog* (a satirical response to [Irish playwright] Samuel Beckett's *Waiting for Godot*), *Les Blancs*, and *What Use Are Flowers?* In 1960, she wrote a television drama entitled *The Drinking Gourd* that had been commissioned by NBC, as part of a special series on the Civil War. Network executives eventually decided it was too violent and divisive for television, however, so it never aired. And in 1961, Hansberry began carrying out a debate about race with writer Norman Mailer in the *Village Voice*.

Illness and Death

By 1963, Hansberry's strength began to deteriorate, and a medical check-up revealed that she was suffering from cancer. Nevertheless, she continued working as much as possible, writing the text for *The Movement: Documentary of a Struggle for Equality*, a photographic history of the civil rights movement prepared by the Student Nonviolent Coordinating Committee. She also began a number of projects that she was ultimately unable to finish, including an epic opera entitled *Toussaint*, about Toussaint L'Ouverture, the late eighteenth-century liberator of Haiti, and an autobiographical novel, *All the Dark and Beautiful Warriors*. In addition, notes found among Hansberry's papers revealed her ideas for a number of other plays, among them one about the Pharaoh Akhenaton, another on eighteenth-century writer Mary Wollstonecraft, one on Native Americans called *Laughing Boy*, and one on African American fiction writer Charles Chesnutt's novel *The Marrow of Tradition*.

The tensions associated with living a very public life—combined, say some sources, with Hansberry's growing awareness of her lesbianism—strained her marriage, and in March 1964 she and Nemiroff divorced. They still maintained a close friendship, however; Nemiroff served as the producer of *The Sign in Sidney Brustein's Window* and stayed with Hansberry in the hospital whenever possible.

In January of 1965, cancer finally claimed Hansberry's life. She had chosen her ex-husband to be the executor of her literary estate, and for the rest of his life, Nemiroff devoted himself to publicizing her works. To that end, he wrote introductions for *A Raisin in the Sun*, arranged for the play's publication, and assembled some of Hansberry's autobiographical writings, plays, and letters to create the drama *To Be Young, Gifted and Black: Lorraine Hansberry in Her Own Words.*

Over 600 people attended Hansberry's funeral in Harlem. During the course of his eulogy, the presiding minister, Eugene Callender, recited messages from James Baldwin and Martin Luther King, Jr. Cheney reprinted the end of King's letter, which read: "Her creative ability and her profound grasp of the deep social issues confronting the world today will remain an inspiration to generations yet unborn."

Hansberry's Life and Work Have Been Misinterpreted

Notable Black American Women

Notable Black American Women is a Gale Research publication featuring biographical profiles of famous black American women.

According to the following selection, one of the great misconceptions about Lorraine Hansberry's life and work is that she was not centrally focused on issues affecting African Americans. This misconception stems from an interview that she gave in which she stated that A Raisin in the Sun *was not a "negro play." By this she meant that the play had universal themes applicable to all peoples, and yet, Hansberry knew well that race could never be divorced from any work about blacks in America. Nevertheless, as the selection points out, Hansberry was a woman of many gifts and many interests, and as much as she was writing about race in America, her plays covered numerous other themes, including sexism, marital and generational conflict, idealism vs. cynicism, women's rights, and the American dream.*

One reason for misinterpretation of Hansberry's life and work is a quote attributed to her by Nan Robertson in a *New York Times* interview about her Broadway hit [*A Raisin in the Sun*], "I told them this wasn't a 'negro play.' It was a play about honest-to-God, believable, many-sided people who happened to be Negroes." This statement, which distorted her real views, was twisted even further by Harold Cruse in his widely read book, *The Crisis of the Negro Intellectual*: "I'm not a Negro writer—but a writer who happens to be a Negro." Hansberry's real position on this question was articulated to interviewer Eleanor Fisher in an attempt to silence these infuriating misrepresentations. She said that "it is impossible to divorce the racial fact from any American Negro." Concerning the family in *A Raisin In the Sun*, she explained to the *New York Times*:

> From the moment the first curtain goes up until they make their decision at the end, the fact of racial oppression, unspoken and unalluded to, other than the fact of how they live, is through the play. It's inescapable. The reason these people are in the ghetto in America is because they are Negroes.

Conflict in *A Raisin in the Sun*

The conflict in *A Raisin in the Sun* at first centers upon what the Younger family will do with ten thousand dollars insurance money their father has left them. He has recently died from overwork and grief from the death of his third child. The eldest child, Walter Lee, wants to invest the money in a liquor store so he can leave his "nothing" job as a white man's chauffeur and go into business. He is obsessed by the idea of money. Walter feels trapped and desperate; Hansberry painted a haunting picture of manhood assaulted by social and economic pressures, and Sidney Poitier gave an electrifying performance that comes across in the film version. Walter Lee's sister, Beneatha, wants to use the money for medical school. In his desperation, Walter Lee has little sympathy for what he thinks is ambition inappropriate for a woman. Mama Lena Younger wishes she could stretch the money to satisfy everybody, but realizes she cannot, so she decides to make a down payment on a house for the family so they will no longer have to put up with high rent and overcrowding. The rest of the money she gives to her son for his business, hoping to alleviate his despair. She asks only that he save some of it for Beneatha's education.

Lena Younger's decision to buy a house in an all-white neighborhood enlarges the initial conflict and eventually unites the family against racism. An emissary from their new neighborhood, Lindner, visits the family and offers to buy their house at a profit for the Youngers if they will not move in. This brings up the theme of restrictive covenants, with which Hansberry was painfully familiar. They refuse his humiliating offer, but then Walter Lee loses all the money given him by Lena Younger to a con artist, and unbeknownst to the rest of the family, calls Lindner back to make the deal, which leads to the climax of the play. Instead of accepting the insulting offer of money, Walter Lee asserts his pride and his manhood by refusing Lindner's deal, and the play ends with the family moving out of the ghetto after all.

No Happy Ending

The critics and audiences interpreted this as a happy ending, amazing Hansberry. She did intend to show the triumph of the human spirit over obstacles, something she believed in and felt that black people were capable of, but the idea that the Youngers' problems were over because they had moved into a white neighborhood was ridiculous to her. Hansberry was well aware of the problems they would be facing and had originally written a fourth act showing the Youngers sitting, armed, in their new house with an angry white mob outside. She cut this act for several reasons—some of them practical: the play ran too long with the extra act, and they needed to save money on the production. Hiring extras would have been an added expense. But the main reason was that she believed in the endurance and the heroism of black people in the face of oppression and that was what she wanted to emphasize. She wanted the audience to see that black Americans wanted change, and that they were brave enough to make it happen. She also wanted white Americans to understand black people, in the hope that fear and ignorance could be removed as obstacles to equal rights.

Hansberry was a Pan-Africanist [a movement to unite those of African descent], but she was never a separatist. She believed that black people should unite and support each other, but she also believed that the dominant culture had to change. She linked the black American struggle to the black African liberation movement in her play through the character of Joseph Asagai, Beneatha's Nigerian suitor. Asagai, who may have been inspired by African students she met through her uncle, Leo Hansberry, is committed to driving out the colonial government in his country. Beneathea decides to marry him and practice medicine in Nigeria. This theme of Pan-Africanism was revolutionary for a play of the time, particularly a Broadway hit, and it introduced these ideas to the American public. Hansberry's thinking on this issue was no doubt influenced by her uncle while she was very young, and she expanded upon it under [American civil rights leader and social commentator] W. E. B. Du Bois at the Jefferson School for Social Science. So close was her association with Du Bois that she was called upon to deliver the eulogy at his funeral.

Hansberry's Universal Themes

There is no doubt that Hansberry's choice of themes for the play make it a drama about the black struggle for liberation. But the play also contains universal themes, among them marital and generational conflict, women's rights, idealism versus cynicism, the American Dream, the dangers of materialism, and Christianity versus atheistic humanism. The play is also very well-constructed, clear and direct, and full of wonderful roles for actors. All these things, including Hansberry's wit, flair for dialogue and stage business, and solid dramaturgy, help locate *A Raisin in the Sun* among the best plays of [the twentieth] century. It opened the door for black Americans in theater and paved the way for the black theater movement of the 1960s and beyond. When pressed in a personal interview, [black American playwright] Ed Bullins admitted that, "Lorraine made a lot of things possible."

Ironically, the white press criticized the play for being a formula money-maker and tried to attribute its success to white liberal guilt over "the Negro question." Representatives from the dominant culture felt free to attack Hansberry for everything and anything related to the issue of racism. In an interview, [*Sixty Minutes* reporter] Mike Wallace grilled her about "Negro anti-Semitism," and tried to blame blacks for the violence in Kenya. Keeping her composure, she replied that it was a mistake to "equalize the oppressed with the oppressor."

Hansberry took strong exception to [French existentialist playwright] Albert Camus's notion of universal guilt and was highly critical of [French existentialist playwright Jean] Genet, [Irish playwright Samuel] Beckett, and the Beat Generation. She felt that their obsession with individual mortality and their idea that real progress is impossible were all luxuries that only self-indulgent intellectuals who were not oppressed could afford. She wrote a hilarious satire of Beckett's *Waiting for Godot* entitled *The Arrival of Mr. Todog* ["Godot" spelled backward] (unpublished), and numerous articles on the subject, including "Genet, Mailer, and the New Paternalism" for the *Village Voice*, and "The Negro Writer and His Roots: Toward a New Romanticism" for the *Black Scholar*. She considered existentialism and the Theatre of the Absurd socially irresponsible, intellectually valueless, and a spiritual dead end.

Alarmed at the vogue these ideas enjoyed among the intellectuals of her age, Hansberry created her second drama, *The Sign In Sidney Brustein's Window*, produced in 1964. It was not nearly the commercial success that her first play had been, for a number of reasons. The intellectual content of the piece was over the heads of most of her audience, and the critics lost patience with it. Even more significantly, critics were frustrated because they could not "type" this playwright. Here was a black woman writing a play about a white male Jewish intellectual. Hansberry disappointed all the people who expected a sequel to *A Raisin in The Sun*, and defied all attempts at classification. She could never limit herself to one issue, one form of expression, or one style of writing. Another reason for its lack of commercial appeal is that its plot is less clear than her first play's, and its structure is sometimes unwieldy. But by the time *Brustein* went into rehearsal, Hansberry was too ill [from cancer] to give her best energy to the arduous process of rewriting that the art of playwriting demands.

Hansberry Is an Inspiration to Later Writers and Activists

Jewelle L. Gomez

Jewelle L. Gomez is a writer and activist and the author of the novel The Gilda Stories *as well as three books of poetry. Her fiction, essays, criticism, and poetry have appeared in numerous periodicals. She also serves as the director of grants and community initiatives for the Horizons Foundation and as president of the San Francisco Public Library Commission.*

In the following selection, Gomez, who, like Lorraine Hansberry, is an African American lesbian writer, pens a moving tribute to her predecessor. Gomez asserts that Hansberry was deeply concerned with numerous social and political concerns and was a warrior in the war of ideas. Her fight against sexism and racism was laudable, and her play A Raisin in the Sun *reflects these concerns. Gomez states that Hansberry serves as an inspiration to activist writers who have come after her. Her caring and commitment and her quest to find universal truths live on in those who have followed in her footsteps.*

I was born on the South Side of Chicago. I was born black and female. I was born in a depression after one world war, and came into my adolescence during another. While I was still in my teens the first atom bombs were dropped on human beings at Nagasaki and Hiroshima. And by the time I was twenty-three years old, my government and that of the Soviet Union had entered actively into the worst conflict of nerves in human history—the Cold War.... I have, like all of you, on a thousand occasions seen indescribable displays of man's very real inhumanity to man, and I have come to

Jewelle L. Gomez, "Lorraine Hansberry: Uncommon Warrior," in *Reading Black, Reading Feminist*, edited by Henry Louis Gates Jr., New York, NY: Meridian, 1990, pp. 307–317. Copyright © Henry Louis Gates, Jr., 1990. All rights reserved. Used by permission of Penguin Group (USA) Inc.

maturity, as we all must, knowing that greed and malice and indifference to human misery and bigotry and corruption, brutality, and perhaps above all else, ignorance—the prime ancient and persistent enemy of man—abound in this world.

I say all of this to say that one cannot live with sighted eyes and feeling heart and not know and react to the miseries which afflict this world.[1]

These words, from a speech Lorraine Hansberry made to a Black writers conference in New York City in 1959, could easily have been those of friends, others I know and work with or even my own. What is most familiar is the sense of disbelief at what we, as humanity, will do to each other, in the name of that same humanity.

These words provide a welcome opportunity to rediscover the depth and breadth of Hansberry's social and political concerns and to see how they are manifest in her work. I say rediscover because today one only need say *Raisin* and the world of her play, *A Raisin in the Sun,* springs fully realized to our minds. It is now easily recalled that she was the first black woman playwright to be produced on Broadway and the youngest ever to win the New York Critics Circle Award. These are statistical triumphs. But in 1959, we more clearly saw the political ramifications of every public black accomplishment. Today Hansberry has entered our consciousness and in some ways that casual acceptance of her success diminishes the social impact of those achievements and their lasting influence on our lives today.

I say rediscover because she was proud of being "young, gifted and Black" at a time when Black women were stereotyped as merely long-suffering matriarchs with sharp tongues. Hansberry's redefinition of black women as active and responsible participants in our political future was surprising in 1959 and remains so to some as we enter the 1990s. It is her pride and the scope of her vision that is the key to her uncommon consciousness. She was truly capable of being a warrior in what Barbara Smith has termed "the most expansive of revolutions."[2] This revolution resists the idea that "one for all and all for me" is a workable attitude. This revolution can no longer focus solely on the wrongs of the past as experienced by one group. That leaves too much room for us to solve our problems and then perpetuate misdeeds against some other group.

As a warrior in this expansive revolution, Hansberry realized that all acts of violence were connected and she did not feel so insecure that the freedom of others frightened her. In fact, she understood that our personal will, our fears, our joys would often be in conflict with our social and political concerns. She was prepared to explore her own insecurities and prejudices in order to confront the larger issues; to confront that system of thinking that had held Black people in subjugation long after slavery was abolished. In rediscovering this warrior waging this expansive revolution I reclaim her as my own. Like all of us, she was more than a snapshot or a bibliography. The legacy she left is that of not only a Black writer but also a political activist and a Black woman. I need her desperately and so should we all.

In the early 1900s actor-singer-minstrel Bert Williams made famous a song entitled "Nobody." It's clear that although the white theater establishment considered that word descriptive of Blacks, Bert Williams did not. He said, "It is no disgrace to be a Negro, but it is very inconvenient."[3] From the nineteenth-century melodramas and minstrel shows to the 1920s musicals like *Shuffle Along*, Black shows were constructed around one premise: Blacks are harmless, not always happy, but definitely as American as pizza pie. While theaters like the Lafayette lit up Harlem with Black stars such as Florence Mills and Charles Gilpin, white audiences, were still intrigued by Ethyl Barrymore in blackface and O'Neill's rendition of the Black experience in *The Emperor Jones*.

Many musicals that originated in Harlem were moved downtown to the big time, making the Depression era one of the largest periods of employment of Black artists on Broadway. The country wanted singing and dancing even when it couldn't afford food! World War II put even greater emphasis on musicals and melodramas, for whites as well as Blacks.

Although the nicest thing that is usually said about the 1950s is that nothing happened, that, in fact, was not true. At the beginning of that decade the most well-known Black dramatic character was still the "mammy" figure embodied by Ethyl Waters in *A Member of the Wedding*, which opened on Broadway in 1950. Langston Hughes was adapting his tales of Semple for the stage; veteran Black actor Canada Lee had just died and his pal, Sidney Poitier, was running a rib joint on 7th Avenue and 131st Street.

Outside the theater, in the daylight, things were not much brighter, but things were happening. Segregation in public schools was being challenged in the courts; citizens were being hauled before the House Un-American Activities Committee (HUAC) and forced to betray their principles and their friends; Japanese-Americans were trying to rebuild their lives after being released from American concentration camps in the Midwest and, as Hansberry noted, the cold war was casting a chilly pall over everything.

It was into this broad arena of change that Lorraine Hansberry stepped. She arrived as an outsider, removed from, but certainly not unaware of, the helter-skelter of Harlem. The great thinkers of her day had been frequent visitors to her childhood home. Her family had lived through the integration of a white neighborhood and her father invested a good bit of his time and professional expertise winning them the right to live anywhere in Chicago that they chose.

Though an outsider, as a writer Hansberry was truly a descendant of the New York writers who came before her. She'd steeped herself in drama from the age of fourteen. She saw as much kinship with the Irish playwrights as with Langston Hughes. She understood the real element of truth in the tired axiom that "people are just people." She saw that in order for a great work to be truly universal it had to be painfully specific. The truth of Black lives had to be explored, not recast into imitations of white life, before Black theater would take its place in world drama. The beginning of the 1950s saw the revival of the 1921 musical hit, *Shuffle Along,* but the end of the decade saw questioning of this simplistic acceptance of Black characters who existed only in relationship to the white world.

What happens to a dream deferred?

Does it dry up

like a raisin in the sun?

Or fester like a sore—

And then run?

Does it stink like rotten meat?

Or crust and sugar over—

like a syrupy sweet?

Maybe it just sags

like a heavy load.

Or does it explode?[4]

These questions posed by Langston Hughes were the same ones that Lorraine Hansberry began to address when her play, "A Raisin in the Sun," opened at the Barrymore Theatre in 1959. She wanted to explore the specifics of Black life; the ideas and urges that fueled our lives politically and personally. She began in a small room, examining it in detail, looking for the universal truth of dignity:

The Younger living room would be a comfortable and well ordered room if it were not for a number of indestructible contradictions to this state of being. Its furnishings are typi-

cal and undistinguished and their primary feature now is
that they have clearly had to accommodate the living of too
many people for too many years and they are tired . . . Wea-
riness has, in fact, won in this room. Everything has been
polished, washed, sat on, used, scrubbed too often. All pre-
tenses but living itself have long since vanished from the
very atmosphere of this room.[5]

She began in a small room with the simple story of a poor
family trying to move into a better neighborhood. The family,
much like her own in spirit, became a symbol of our aspirations. But as a writer, Hansberry's work is even bigger than
that. She arrived at a pivotal point in the development of
Black drama and Black thinking. She believed, as many were
just beginning to, in probing the specifics of her characters by
peeling back the generalities, whether those generalities were
culture, ethnicity, gender or language. She was convinced that
beneath any combination of these elements was a distinct human being who, given a voice, would make a valid statement
about humankind.

Raisin opened up the questions of the validity of middle
class aspirations; the right of women to control their own
bodies and their intellectual independence; the inherent con-
servatism of the underclasses; the myth of the Black matriarch; the connection between Africans and Afro-Americans;
some of which were issues not being raised by Blacks in public. In the 1960 some implied Hansberry's inadequacy as a
spokesperson for the black revolution by saying she was too
middle class, mistakenly assuming that socioeconomic status
and personality are as immutable as race. It ignored the fact
that many major social revolutionaries have risen from the
middle classes: Gandhi, Marx, Ho Chi Minh, Nkrumah, Castro, King.

Hansberry was able to create substantial characters who
lived and *grew*. The Younger family symbolized the opposing
systems of thought that continue to tear this country apart,

each character individually, and the family as a whole. It was not just a matter of house versus liquor store; Mama's dream versus Walter Lee's dream. The contest was also between the individual and the collective good. This was not a play simply about upward mobility or integration.

Many critics have neglected the full ramifications of Hansberry's life as a cultural worker. Her plays, the product of a young and diligent mind, work dramaturgically within the context of the drama of her day. When she arrived, American theater had fallen, head first, into the pit of naturalism, reducing plays from poetry to newspaper clippings. She was working in one medium (playwriting) which was taking its shape from another (fiction writing) and it was doing so poorly. Drama left the realm of wonder where it had begun: the church and the ritual that was its birthplace. It moved into an undefined arena where its artists were filled with self-consciousness about their craft. They sought legitimacy in staid presentations of "reality" rather than continuing the tradition of the transportation of the heart and soul.

Hansberry took that naturalistic style and deliberately infused it with an array of ideas, which other writers were consciously not doing. Beyond the message that Black is now real and good, there was no other dimension to the political and social concepts of Black drama. Hansberry was an intensely political person.

Once proclaimed the reigning queen of Black drama, Hansberry did not let up. In her next play, "The Sign in Sidney Brustein's Window," she had the audacity to make the central characters white! The play's production met [with] scorn from both white and Black critics. This in spite of the fact that white people had been describing and defining Black people for centuries, not only on paper but in real life. The play also included a gay male character, but people were not interested in talking about him at all, much less demanding Hansberry's qualifications to describe him.

Lorraine Hansberry accepts an award for best drama for her play A Raisin in the Sun. *The first black female playwright to be produced on Broadway, Lorraine Hansberry was an activist as well as a writer.* AP Images.

Lorraine Hansberry had many stories to tell. She did not feel the need to justify any one of them. She had strong concerns for many issues affecting this society and did not cower in the shadow of political repression that loomed over the 1950s. In 1957, Hansberry flew to a peace congress in Uruguay to deliver a speech in place of Paul Robeson, whose passport had been revoked. When she returned, the United States government revoked her passport.

In 1957, when the leader of the first gay male organization, The Mattachine Society, had already been called before the HUAC, along with a number of "suspected" homosexuals,

Hansberry still espoused human rights. At the same time she wrote a letter to *The Ladder*, the first journal published for lesbians in this country. She said: "It is time that 'half the human race' had something to say about the nature of its existence . . . In this kind of work there may be women to emerge who will be able to formulate a new and possible concept that homosexual persecution and condemnation has at its roots not only social ignorance but a philosophically active antifeminist dogma."[6]

Anticipating the modern feminist movement, she wrote in 1957: "Woman, like the Negro, like the Jew, like colonial peoples, even in ignorance, is incapable of accepting the role with harmony. This is because it is an unnatural role. The station of woman is hardly one that she would assume by choice, any more than men would. It must necessarily be imposed on her by force . . . A status not freely chosen or entered into by an individual or group is necessarily one of oppression and the oppressed are by their nature . . . forever in ferment and agitation against their condition and what they understand to be their oppressors. If not by overt rebellion or revolution, then in the thousand and one ways they will devise with and without consciousness to alter their condition."[7]

Because Hansberry has been regarded only within the light of Black (mostly male) dramatists her larger context as a woman has been ignored. Discussion of *Raisin* is most often centered around Walter Lee and his frustrations or his conflict with his mother. The character frequently overlooked is Beneatha, Walter Lee's sister and the most autobiographical of Hansberry's characters. Early in *A Raisin in the Sun* Beneatha has this exchange with the African who is pushing her to marry him:

> *Beneatha*: You never understood that there is more than one kind of feeling which can exist between a man and a woman—or, at least, there should be.

Asagai (Shaking his head negatively but gently): No. Between a man and a woman there need be only one kind of feeling. I have that for you . . .

Beneatha: I know—and by itself—it won't do. I can find that anywhere.

Asagai: For a woman it should be enough.

Beneatha: I know—because that's what it says in all the novels that men write. But it isn't.[8]

These words were not put in the mouth of Walter Lee's sister merely to show her as rebellious and troublesome. These were the political beliefs of Lorraine Hansberry. In some unpublished notes she examines the idea that "feminine" traits, such as love, compassion, and understanding, are reserved for only woman's personality. She wrote: "This is the supreme insult against men. Is it only woman who truly possesses the most magnificent features of the human race—I a woman think not—and it is time men decided it is the great slander of the ages—to take our hands—truly—as comrades."[9]

As clearly as she understood the nature of relationships between women and men, she saw the relationships between nations. She foresaw that the betrayal of the Cuban Revolution would come from the U.S. Government, not from Fidel Castro, and said so in the *New York Times*.[10] She understood that colonialism was breaking the backs of people of color, not unlike herself, and said so in her play *Les Blancs*. She understood Zora Neale Hurston's comment that Black women are the mules of the world and she refused to be one and said so every opportunity she had.

Because we have not studied Hansberry as a cultural worker and thinker but only as a dramatist, we have lost touch with the urgency of her political message and the poetry of her writing, in particular her prose. In an essay for Broadway's *Playbill* magazine, she wrote:

> I remember being startled when I first saw my grandmother rocking away on her porch. All my life I had heard that she was a great beauty and no one had ever remarked that they meant a half century before. The woman I met was as wrinkled as a prune and could hardly hear and barely see and always seemed to be thinking of other times. But she could still rock and talk and even made wonderful cupcakes which were like cornbread only sweet. She died the next summer and that is all that I remember about her, except that she was born in slavery and had memories of it and they didn't sound anything like *Gone With the Wind*.[11]

Just as her grandmother's memories were able to shed light on the past and reshape her thinking about the Black reality, Hansberry is able to look again at our lives as women and shine a light on them so we remember what it was really supposed to be about.

Hansberry's unfinished novel, *All the Dark and Beautiful Warriors*,[12] has not been published but it was excerpted in the *Village Voice*. The depth of her perception about women and men, their roles in society (Black and white), and the love with which she communicates this understanding are undeniable. The issues of class, sexism, and racism are addressed more adroitly in a few paragraphs of this unfinished work than in a good number of the volumes produced by the protests of the 1960s Black Nationalist movement.

There are several aspects to the tragedy of the loss of Lorraine Hansberry. She was not only a young woman, thirty-four years old, but a young writer. Her talent, her style, her ideas were being shaped by her just-beginning uncommon political consciousness. She was a young warrior in this "most expansive of revolutions." Yet she acknowledged that there is a unified system of thought that allows little Black girls to be blown to bits in Birmingham; that allows the flesh of Jews to be turned into lampshades; that allows generations of an indigenous people to be decimated in a place that is called the land of the free. It is a unified system of thinking that demands that women who have been raped justify their anger; that allows a man to do less time in prison than if he'd robbed a bank, although he's killed a public official. This system of thought decrees that this travesty is justice if the victim happens to be Jewish or gay.

Hansberry had considered all of these political issues and taken a solid position that their resolutions were interdependent. She would have been invaluable in the great divisive debate about whether or not Black women need feminism. In *Ebony* magazine in 1963 she wrote:

> It is indeed a single march, a unified destiny and the prize is the future. In the ascent we shall want and need to lose some of the features of our collective personality for which we are justly ill-famed; but it is also to be hoped that we shall cling just as desperately to certain others for which we are not less harshly criticized. For above all, in behalf of an ailing world which sorely needs our defiance, may we as Negroes or women never accept the notion of—"our place."[13]

As a Black woman, a writer, and a lesbian-feminist, I need Lorraine Hansberry so that her brilliant vision lights my path. For by leaving us her notebooks and fragments of work, she has created an invaluable wealth of energy and resources for me as I search for the tradition of Black women writers and thinkers into which I properly fit.

Etched on the marble stone of her grave are these words from her play, *The Sign in Sidney Brustein's Window*: "I care. I care about it all. It takes too much energy not to care... The why of why we are here is an intrigue for adolescents; the how is what must command the living. Which is why I have lately become an insurgent again."[14]

She has lately become an insurgent again, inside of me. I felt her moving me to action as I prepared this work. But she predicted that, too. She knew that people/women would study the specifics of her life and find the universal truths we needed and that we would claim her. During her last days she dictated her feelings and ideas into a tape recorder. At the end she said: "If anything should happen—before 'tis done—may I trust that all commas and periods will be placed and someone will complete my thoughts—This last should be the least difficult—since there are so many who think as I do."[15]

She was right, again.

Notes

1. From a speech delivered at a Black writers' conference in 1959. Cited in *To Be Young, Gifted, and Black*, adapted by Robert Nemiroff. (New York: New American Library, 1969), 41.

2. Barbara Smith, "Toward a Black Feminist Criticism," *Conditions: Two* (October 1977) 42–47.

3. Loften Mitchell, *Black Drama* (New York: Hawthorne Books, 1967), 49.

4. Langston Hughes, "Montage of a Dream Deferred," in *Selected Poems/Langston Hughes* (New York: Vintage Books, 1974), 268.

5. Lorraine Hansberry, *A Raisin in the Sun* (New York: New American Library of World Literature, 1959), 11–12.

6. See Jonathan Katz, *Gay American History* (New York: Thomas Y. Crowell, 1976), 425.

7. See Adrienne Rich, "The Problem with Lorraine Hansberry," *Freedomways*, Vol. 19, Number 4 (1979), 253.

8. Hansberry, *op. cit.*, 50.

9. Lorraine Hansberry's unpublished, untitled notes, New York City, November 16, 1955. As quoted in Margarte Wilkerson, "Lorraine Hansberry: The Complete Feminist," *Freedomways*, Vol. 19 (Number 4, 1979), 244.

10. Lorraine Hansberry, "Village Intellect Revealed," *New York Times*, 31 October 1964, section 2, 3.

11. Lorraine Hansberry, "On Summer," *Playbill* (June 27, 1960), 27.

12. Lorraine Hansberry, *All Dark and Beautiful Warriors,* unpublished. Excerpted in the *Village Voice,* 16 August 1983, with introduction by Thulani Davis.

13. Lorraine Hansberry, "This Complex of Womanhood," *Ebony* (September 1963).

14. Lorraine Hansberry, *The Sign in Sidney Brustein's Window,* quoted in the preface to Anne Cheney, *Lorraine Hansberry* (Boston: Twayne Publishers, 1984).

15. *To Be Young, Gifted, and Black,* adapted by Robert Nemiroff. (New York: New American Library, 1969), 265.

A Raisin in the Sun and Gender

A *Raisin in the Sun* Depicts Complicated Male and Female Family Relationships

Geneviève Fabre

Geneviève Fabre is Professor Emerita of American literature at the University of Paris. She has written and edited numerous books on African American culture and literature and has received several prestigious fellowships.

In the following viewpoint, Fabre looks at Lorraine Hansberry's A Raisin in The Sun *through the lens of family interactions and suggests that the play resists stereotypes about black families that so often oversimplify complex problems. Fabre sees* Raisin *as the most interesting portrayal of an African American family to appear on the stage and credits this realistic depiction to Hansberry's creation of complex interfamilial relationships. Hansberry's female characters are generous, strong women, and yet they are also culpable in hindering Walter's development as a man. This contradictory depiction is one of the play's strengths as a document of African American life, Fabre believes.*

The Family: Hero or Anti-Hero

"Expert" studies of the black family such as the Moynihan Report describe the persistent failure of blacks to create stable family units;[29] if the entire society depends on the institution of the family, then the "deterioration of the black family" leads to the demise of the community. Paradoxically, the benevolent attitude of liberal scholars toward blacks has led to the same conclusion. The stereotypes have only been rationalized and the image remains negative. The Moynihan Report is a startling example of the way white liberals have tried to legislate on behalf of the black community while remaining ignorant of its culture and social fabric. Black theatre could neither ignore these attitudes nor remain apart from the debate; indeed, the issues theatre tries to raise are central to the whole question of the black family.

The debate follows two different paths. The liberal approach shows how the black family conformed to models of white society and attributes its alienation to socioeconomic factors that handicap blacks. The other approach seeks neither to rehabilitate nor to explain, but to present the family as a group of individuals both united by ties that have nothing to do with legality and profoundly divided by conflicts. The family appears as a dynamic unit, a cultural entity gifted with its own vitality; what must be dramatized are the dialectical relations it maintains with other elements of the community and with the dominant society.[30]

Undoubtedly, Lorraine Hansberry's *A Raisin in the Sun* (see Chapter 1) provides the most interesting prototype of the black family ever developed in contemporary theatre. It has served as a paradigm for a whole series of representations, in which this model is sometimes amplified and diversified, sometimes radically contested.

Hansberry endows the Younger family with characteristics that stem from contradictory intentions. She sets out to challenge existing stereotypes by retracing the important episodes in the history of this exemplary family. However, the situations in which the Youngers are placed and their behavior show them to be exceptional and separate from the mass of family "types" in the ghetto. Instead of destroying the stereotype, the play only shows how the Youngers escaped it.

Like those of many Afro-Americans, the Youngers' forebears left for the North in search of employment and a life free from racism. Just as in *Our Lan'* by Theodore Ward, the family epic begins with dreams and hopes, despite inevitable setbacks. In the Chicago ghetto, the Youngers subsist in poverty. One is tempted to see the absence of the father as typical desertion until it is learned that the head of the family is dutifully dead. To make the relations between the characters more dramatic, Hansberry introduces a moment of crisis when each dreams of spending the dead father's insurance annuity in his or her own way. The different aspirations reveal diverging ethical choices and become sources of conflict. The daughter wants to continue her medical studies; the mother wants to buy a house in a white suburb; Walter, the son, wants to open a liquor store. Concerned about respectability, Mrs. Younger opposes Walter's project and forbids him to accept a deal offered by their prospective neighbors who want to keep blacks out of the neighborhood. No doubt, *Raisin* illustrates the social and racial relations in America, which promises integration in theory only. On a more profound level, however, the Youngers' victory is due to the fact that they are different from others in the ghetto: they "deserve" to move into the white suburbs because they have adopted the values of the middle class that they hope to join. Hansberry's hope for integration for the Youngers and for black theatre can pass as a concession to the tastes and ideology of Broadway audiences. The Younger family's aspirations—to get out of the ghetto at all costs, to satisfy basic needs and eventually "plant a garden"—characterize many ghetto families. But the Youngers' entry into an all-white neighborhood does not portend a bright future. Perhaps it is on this point that the play is dishonest: in its depiction of integration as salvation and in its happy ending.

The test of blacks desiring to integrate a white neighborhood at the end of the fifties is depicted somewhat more realistically in *Take a Giant Step* By Louis Peterson. This play can serve as a follow-up to *Raisin*, since it shows the life of a black family after the move. Yet neither Hansberry nor Peterson states openly that integration is often a trap for blacks. In effect, if social mobility allows them either by accident or by exception to better their condition, it also leads them into a hostile environment and exiles them from their community.[31]

Raisin, however, marks an important step in the direction black theatre will take in its image of the family. The play sets characters in specific roles that serve as a basic pattern: dominant women and unscrupulous, immoral, or ineffectual men. Constantly nagged by the women in his family, Walter serves as a scapegoat for their frustrations. In a world of criminals and victims, possessors and the possessed, he wants to possess, not for respectability but out of a need for independence. Walter's complaint is that of the black man who forever endures the harassment of a society that leaves him nothing but dreams, and the nagging of women in his family who do not want him to dream. The opposition among the characters expresses an opposition among value systems: conflicts between the mother (work ethic and merit) and the son (materialism, success that comes from money); conflict between brother and sister (who wants an education and who substitutes African references for the American Dream). Yet the play's interest lies especially in the representation of relations between the man and the woman and in the contradictory images Hansberry proposes. The portrait of the mother underscores the qualities of honesty and endurance, but Walter points out the way the woman begrudges her companion the respect and attention he needs:

Man say to his woman, I got me a dream. His woman say: Eat your eggs. Man say I got to take hold of this here world baby. And a woman will say: Eat your eggs and go to work. Man say: I got to change my life, I'm choking to death, baby! And his woman say—Your eggs is getting cold . . . That is just what is wrong with the colored woman in this world . . . Don't understand about building their men up and making 'em feel like they somebody. Like they can do something.[32]

One cannot ignore this criticism of the down-to-earth woman who keeps her man from dreaming and realizing his dreams, criticism that is presented alongside the image of the generous, strong woman who cements family unity. In the theatre of the sixties this role will be more clearly defined as a castrator, and the woman will appear quite often as the major obstacle to the man's affirmation of virility. . . .

Notes

29. *The Negro Family: The Case for National Action* (Washington, D.C.: U.S. Government Printing Office, March 1965). This report has been analyzed and criticized in Lee Rainwater and William C. Yancey, eds., *The Moynihan Report and the Politics of Controversy* (Cambridge: MIT Press, 1967).

30. After so many rash generalizations about the black family, Herbert Gutman's *The Black Family in Slavery and Freedom, 1750–1925* (New York: Pantheon, 1976) shows the important role the family played in the history and development of black culture. Following the work of black sociologist E. Franklin Frazier, *The Negro Family* (1939) , Gutman emphasizes the existence of a complex cultural network in which the family plays a determinant role. Frazier maintained that the socioeconomic conditions forced upon blacks had helped to destroy the family. For Gutman, the black family not only survived but served several functions and was a dynamic element in the cultural life of the community.

31. Ironically, in *Raisin* blacks could only afford housing in the white neighborhood, for costs were prohibitive in black sectors. Houses in the ghetto were too run-down to provide decent lodging. In one sense, the deal Mrs. Younger

struck for the house is just as dangerous as the business deal Walter proposed; she merely moves her family from one ghetto to another. The play refuses to go a step further to show the consequences of Mrs. Younger's generous obstinacy or the life of her family condemned to exile.

32. Hansberry, *A Raisin in the Sun*, p. 22.

Hansberry Depicts the Struggle of an Emasculated Male Hero

C.W.E. Bigsby

C.W.E. Bigsby is professor of American studies at the University of East Anglia, in Norwich, England. He is also director of the Arthur Miller Centre for American Studies there. He has published nearly forty books, including four novels.

In the following selection, Bigsby explains that both Richard Wright, in his novel Native Son, *and Lorraine Hansberry, in* A Raisin in the Sun, *depict the struggle of an emasculated black male. But while protagonist Bigger Thomas in Wright's novel is a victim of the inexorability of his fate, Walter Lee Younger becomes aware of dreams beyond the purely material. Bigsby argues that Walter Lee's cynicism is balanced by the idealism of his sister Beneatha and of her African suitor, Joseph Asagai. Yet even while the Youngers commit to a new, ennobled level of struggle, Bigsby writes, the play depends on an artificial and unconvincing resolution. Asagai's belief in the inevitability of change based on courage and compassion remains unconvincing, as does Walter's change of heart at the end of the play.*

Lorraine Hansberry's first play, *A Raisin in the Sun*, was awarded the New York Drama Critics' Prize for 1959–60. For all its sympathy, humour and humanity, however, it remains disappointing—the more so when compared with the achievement of her second play, *The Sign in Sidney Brustein's Window*. Yet it passes considerably beyond the trivial music-hall dramas of [African American writer] Langston Hughes

C.W.E. Bigsby, *Confrontation and Commitment: A Study of Contemporary American Drama 1959–66*, Columbia, MO: University of Missouri Press, 1968, pp. 156–161. Copyright © 1967 and 1968 by C.W.E. Bigsby. All rights reserved. Reproduced by permission.

and does something to capture the sad dilemma of Negro and white alike without lapsing into the bitter hatred of Richard Wright or the psychodrama of [Irish American playwright Eugene] O'Neill's *All God's Chillun Got Wings*. Its weakness is essentially that of much Broadway naturalism [a literary movement that stressed how environment shaped character]. It is an unhappy crossbreed of social protest and re-assuring resolution. Trying to escape the bitterness of Wright, Hansberry betrays herself into radical simplification and ill-defined affirmation. Like [American novelist] Saul Bellow she senses the validity of affirmation before she can justify it as a logical implication of her play's action.

"The Demoralisation of the Black Male"

A Raisin in the Sun is set in Chicago's Southside 'sometime between World War II and the present'. The Younger family live in a roach-infested building so overcrowded that they have to share the bathroom with another family while Travis, the only son of Walter and Ruth Younger, has to sleep on a sofa in the living room. Yet the central factor of the play is not poverty but indignity and self-hatred. The survival of the family is dependent on their ability to accommodate themselves to the white world. Walter works as a chauffeur while his wife works as a maid. To both of them accommodation to the point of servility is required for the very right to work. [African American novelist] James Baldwin has indicated the cost to the individual of accepting one's life on another's terms, 'one of the prices an American Negro pays—or can pay—for what is called his "acceptance" is a profound, almost ineradicable self hatred'. *A Raisin in the Sun* is primarily a study of such self-hatred, emphasised here, as Baldwin saw it emphasised in an article called 'Alas, Poor Richard', by a confrontation between the enervated American Negro and the dignified self-confidence of the African.

There is a story by Richard Wright called 'Man of All Work' in which a Negro man dresses up as a woman in order to get work as a cook. His action emphasises what Baldwin has called 'the demoralisation of the Negro male' when his position as breadwinner is necessarily usurped by the woman. It is this agony with which Walter Younger lives. He has been desexualised and his dignity has been crushed. It is this knowledge which underlies his bitter disgust and self-contempt. 'I'm thirty-five years old; I been married eleven years and I got a boy who sleeps in the living room—and all I got to give him is stories about how rich white people live'. When a ten thousand dollar insurance matures on his father's death he has to watch the money pass into his mother's hands—a final blow to both his dreams and his manhood. '*You* the head of this family. You run our lives like you want to'.

Hansberry vs. Richard Wright

Richard Wright, sensing the emasculation of the Negro trapped in the physical ghetto of Chicago and the cage of self-contempt alike, had seen in violence both the Negro's attempt to re-assert himself and an expression of white oppression. Bigger Thomas, who kills, decapitates and incinerates a white woman, thereby achieves a measure of self-awareness which had previously escaped him. Hansberry's play is set in the same locale. Its sense of desperation is the same. Walter Younger's emasculation is pushed to the point at which he condones his wife's attempt to secure an abortion. Yet where Wright created in Bigger Thomas a hardening of the stereotype, which was in effect a spring-board for an exegesis of communist doctrine, Hansberry, writing some twenty years later, is concerned with demonstrating human resilience. The gulf between the two writers is in part that dictated by the changing social position of the American Negro but more fundamentally it is indicative of Lorraine Hansberry's belief in the pointlessness of despair and hatred. Indeed Hansberry's play is essentially an attempt to turn Wright's novel on its head. Where he had examined the potential for violence, Hansberry sees this as a potential which once realised can only lead to stasis. Both works start with an alarm-clock ringing in the stifling atmosphere of Chicago's coloured ghetto. Yet whereas Bigger Thomas wakes up to the inexorability of his fate, Walter becomes conscious of the existence of other levels than the purely material. The sense of urgency presaged by the initial alarm is as much the key-note of Hansberry's play as it is of Wright's novel yet while the alarm functions as a threat in the latter it functions as a promise in the former.

A Family's Dreams

The play's title is taken from a poem by Langston Hughes—a poem which expresses the sense of kinetic energy and tension which underlies the frustrations of the American Negro, an energy which can be turned into violence, self-destruction, despair or genuine realisation:

What happens to a dream deferred?

Does it dry up

Like a raisin in the sun?

Or fester like a sore—

And then run?

Does it stink like rotten meat?

Or crust and sugar over—

Like a syrupy sweet?

Maybe it just sags

Like a heavy load.

Or does it explode?

The dreams of the Youngers are sharpened and pointed by the indignity and self-hatred which is their racial inheritance.

Walter dreams of owning a store and thus becoming independent of the system of which he is the victim, while his sister-
in-law, impressed by the need for compassion, wants to become a doctor. Lena Younger, Walter's mother, however, is
concerned only with the disintegration of the family. When
the money arrives she places a deposit on a new house. The
decision drives Walter into a despairing disaffiliation.

Walter Younger's sullen cynicism, which, like Willy Loman's
confused mind in [Arthur Miller's] *Death of a Salesman,* grants
value only to wealth and power, is balanced by his sister-in-
law's passionate belief in the feasibility of change and the need
for compassion. Beneatha has a strong sense of racial pride
compounded with humanistic commitment. Intensely aware
of her racial origins she associates with Asagai, an African student, and steeps herself in the culture of her forbears. When
Asagai gives her the nickname Alaiyo, 'one who needs more
than bread', it is both an ironical comment on her intensity
and an indication that Hansberry's concern is less with the
poverty of the Youngers than with the need for spiritual re-
plenishment which can only come with a return of dignity.
Yet when Walter squanders the money which was to have paid
for her medical training, Beneatha lapses into despair and the
compassion which she had shown evaporates as had Ruth's
hope and Walters's ambitions. Like Sidney Brustein in
Hansberry's second play, forced to confront present reality, she
slips into the cant of nihilism [philosophy that stresses the
meaninglessness of life]. She projects her personal disappoint-
ments onto a universal scale and Asagai identifies the questions which obsess her. 'What good is struggle; what good is
anything? Where are we all going? And why are we bothering?'

The personal and familial crises are finally resolved by the
open challenge offered by the white world. Karl Lindner, whose
name suggests non-American origins, is the representative of
the white community into which the family had planned to
move. He offers to buy the house from them at a profit. The

insult is delivered with courtesy but it stings Walter into a response which simultaneously gives him back his dignity and commits him to an involvement which he had sought to escape. Thus in a sense this is a fulfilment of Asagai's prophecy. In speaking of his own political future in Africa he had said, 'They who might kill me even . . . actually replenish me!'

An Artificial Resolution

Yet while leaving the Youngers committed to [what Robert Nemiroff described as] 'new levels of struggle' Miss Hansberry brings about this partial resolution through something of a specious *deus ex machina*. Although she is as antipathetic towards a life printed on dollar bills as [America's playwright Clifford] Odets had been, it is clear that the spiritual regeneration of the Younger family is ultimately contingent on a ten thousand dollar check, for it is only the money which makes it possible for them to challenge the system under which they have suffered. In making it the necessary prerequisite for their return to dignity and pride Hansberry would seem to demean the faith in human potential which she is ostensibly endorsing. Walter, again like Willy Loman, far from rejecting the system which is oppressing him, wholeheartedly embraces it. He rejects the cause of social commitment and compassion and places his faith in the power of money. It is the unintentional irony of this play, however, that he proves to be right, 'You all want everybody to carry a flag and a spear and sing some marching songs, huh? You wanna spend your life looking into things and trying to find the right and the wrong part . . . There ain't no causes—there ain't nothing but taking in this world, and he who takes most is smartest—and it don't make a damn bit of difference how.' Without the insurance check not only would the dreams have been left to shrivel like raisins in the sun but so would Beneatha's compassion and Walter's courage. Indeed Walter's final conversion, or, as Hansberry would put it, the eventual realisation of his potential, is itself as unconvincing as Biff's similar conversion in *Death of a Salesman*. Her true declaration of faith is, however, embodied in the person of Asagai, the least convincing of the play's characters. This African revolutionary is used by Lorraine Hansberry as a point of reference—as the realisation of the dignity and commitment which exists in Walter only as potential. When Walter, returning home drunk, had leapt onto a table and shouted out the words of a defiant nationalism, he had been establishing a contact with the African which served at the same time as a source of contrast and promise. Yet Asagai's self-assurance remains untested. His confident assertion of progress and redemption remains unreal precisely because we do not see him, as we do the Youngers, brought face to face with frustration.

The relationship between the American Negro and the African remains, as Baldwin had in part anticipated it would, a complex arrangement of subtle misunderstandings. Particularly in the nineteen-twenties' 'Negro Renaissance' Africa was seen as a pagan but innocent land. In a poem by [African American writer] Gwendolyn Bennett the sense of a corrupted present is emphasised by a romantic longing for an African past in which identity was more than a response to a hostile environment:

I want to see lithe Negro girls,

Etched dark against the sky

While Sunset lingers.

I want to hear the silent sands,

Singing to the moon

Before the Sphinx-still face . . .

I want to hear the chanting

Around a heathen fire

Of a strange black race.

I want to breathe the Lotus flow'r,

Sighing to the stars

With tendrils drinking at the Nile.

I want to feel the surging

Of my sad people's soul

Hidden by a minstrel-smile.

And again the same contrast in 'No Images' by [African American poet] Waring Cuney:

She does not know

Her beauty,

She thinks her brown body

Has no glory.

If she could dance

Naked,

Under the palm trees

And see her image in the river

She would know.

But there are no palm trees

On the street,

And dishwater gives back no images.

An Unconvincing Ending

While this romantic view of Africa repelled both the Christian and the communist whose approach to that continent was coloured by their own ideology, it was a view which seems to have seized the imagination of many writers. It is certainly clear that *A Raisin in the Sun* accepts unquestioningly the validity of Cuney's symbol. Asagai has no validity outside of this convention. If Hansberry mocks the naïvete with which Beneatha tries to adopt African modes of dress and general culture, she leaves unchallenged the assumption that those values stem from a purer source. Yet Asagai's vitality and enthusiasm spring from his own dreams, which differ in kind from Walter's only in magnitude and in the fact that they are never put to the test. We see Walter balance his manhood against a dream of success but Asagai remains nothing but an oracle whose declarations make sense only to those who are faithful to the stereotyped African of Bennett and Cuney, rich in wisdom and standing, like the noble savage, as a reminder of primal innocence. Asagai's declaration of the inevitability of change built on courage and compassion, a declaration which clearly represents Lorraine Hansberry's own faith, remains as unconvincing as do the circumstances of Walter's change of heart, 'things will happen, slowly and swiftly. At times it will seem that nothing changes at all ... and then again ... the sudden dramatic events which make history leap into the future. And then quiet again ... And I even will have moments when I wonder if the quiet was not better than all that death and hatred. But ... I will not wonder long.'

Walter Must Reclaim His Role as Family Head

Paul Carter Harrison

Paul Carter Harrison is an American playwright and emeritus literature professor. His books include Black Light: The African American Hero *and* Black Theatre: Ritual Performance in the African Diaspora.

In the following selection, Harrison argues that white critics have tended to view black plays according to their own sociological frame of reference, not recognizing the unique life force that is particular to those of African descent. Thus they see A Raisin in the Sun *as a play about a power struggle between the women in the family and Walter. In reality, Harrison contends, Walter has been stripped of his patriarchal status by the forces of white oppression rather than by his own women. It is Lena who, harnessing the male principle derived from her dead husband, attempts to restore Walter to his rightful place as family head using the power of "Nommo," the African concept that defines the human body and mind as being one with the life force, in rhythm with the earth and their African ancestors. Lorraine Hansberry thus confirms the spiritual health of the Younger family, Harrison writes, but fails artistically by trying to force an artificially happy ending.*

Until recently, it was difficult to truly authenticate the black theater because the black experience was constantly being defined in sociological terms. Sociological method allows whites an easy handle on the descriptive life of blacks. Thus, having bought the pre-packaged image, many black artists ignored the forces of life and found themselves scraping

the bottom of the slice-of-life bag for pieces of the black experience to authenticate—perhaps for sentimental reasons—our
existence. The resulting product was often a eunuch's simu-
lacrum of white culture which, as [African American play-
wright] Imamu Baraka teaches, is "at best, corny." We are en-
tertained, perhaps, but we learn nothing, since the spirit
remains frozen, the potency of our being seldom ignited,
much less regenerated. The spiritual release required to reveal
the mode is subverted by mechanical manipulation of the
content of black experience. Form, as understood by Western
standards, locks the spirit into a box in order to suppress the
emergence of a vision that might be too potent to handle;
content then becomes subordinate to its almost anal-sphincter
control.

If an event is to have dramatic force and verity, it requires
the psychic/physical energies of all assembled—as in the ritual
of a voodoo ceremony—to be fused into a dynamic unity so
as to mutually achieve a spontaneous suspension of disbelief.
Black people, owing to African continuity, are not spectators
by nature; they are participators. The images created in an
event gain in spiritual and physical potency through active
participation in the mode. . . .

Spiritual life is an inextricable element of black community life. And Nommo force [life force derived from African
ancestry] is the great orginizer. Society is the natural way
Nommo exerts itself. Society is the highest manifestation of
Nommo. The power that holds the family together is Nommo
force in operation, however corruptive the force of oppression
may have been. The spiritual position of the members of the
family become manifest, thus mother and father enjoy a hierarchy within the family beyond their biological existence. . . .

By sociological definition, Lorraine Hansberry's *Raisin In
The Sun* seems superficially contrived to show the efforts of a
castrated black man to overcome his mother's dominance over
a family striving for middle-class respectability without the

cohesive force of a father, who is dead. In traditional societies, the male is recognized as a dominant force in the family, and thus in the community. However, his role does not limit the mother's naturally endowed force, which is viewed as being akin to the power of nature. While her force is never questioned, her role within the family is designated by the man, since it is the man who determines the community life-style. They mutually and unquestioningly understand their relationships to the social dynamics of the life mode, or, rather, to the force field. However much man may be a dominant force, a severe shift in the mode may forbid him dominance over the new forces.

When a man loses his sense of malehood, the entire community is castrated. White oppression in America has proven to be an insidious force since it constantly attacks the masculinity of the black community. The traditional matri-focal relationship has been shaken out of focus, and suddenly becomes a complex, a *condition*, an unnatural product of that assault. When a man is not able to designate his *own* goals, he cannot be considered a determining force in the life-style of his community. Women then are obliged to shoulder greater responsibilities. Still, it would be fallacious to assume that the matriarchal syndrome among blacks results from a male-female conflict. It is, rather, the direct result of oppression, which has forged conditions that create the appearance of such conflicts.

Family

Despite Hansberry's obvious misrepresentation of the black family's aspirations in a socio-realistic play which, at best, gives only a linear description of the forces of oppression, she demonstrates a profound understanding of how a family is spiritually cemented. With naturalistic detail, she orders the principal Kintu—money—into its proper relationship to the family's oppression. And when money exerts its force, threat-

In this scene from the 1961 film adaption of A Raisin in the Sun, *Walter (Sidney Poitier) cowers beneath the dominance of his mother (Claudia McNeil). Critics contend that Walter's struggle to fulfill his role as the head of the household parallels the black community's fight against white oppression.* © Bettmann/Corbis.

ening to split up the family, she has the mother Nommo [push] the *male principle* forward into its rightful, symbolic position in the family by giving her son, Walter Lee, the money from an insurance policy, the spiritual legacy of the dead father:

MAMA:

Walter—what you ain't never understood is that I ain't got nothing, don't own nothing, ain't never really wanted nothing that wasn't for you. There ain't nothing as precious to me . . . There ain't nothing worth holding on to, money, dreams, nothing else—if it means—if it means it's going to destroy my boy. (*gives money*) It ain't much, but it's all I got in the world and I'm putting it in your hands. I'm telling you to be the head of this family from now on like you supposed to be.

And later, after the money has been squandered in an unaccomplished bit of *slick*, the mother urges forth the most potent force she can conjure—the spirit of the father—to harmonize the mode of her rage:

MAMA:

I seen . . . him . . . night after night . . . come in . . . and look at that rug . . . and then look at me . . . the red showing in his eyes . . . the veins moving in his head . . . I seen him grow thin and old before he was forty . . . working and working and working like somebody's old horse . . . killing himself . . . and you—you give it all away in a day . . . Oh God . . . Look down here . . . and show me the strength . . . strength . . . strength!

Hansberry uses, without conscious contrivance—it is more like *ubengwe* [creative intelligence]—the rhythmic pulse and repetition of an incantation to allow the mother to invoke the spirit of the *male principle* which guides her wisdom and gives her strength for clearer action.

An Inappropriate Happy Ending

In African thought, it is not necessary to speak of forming unions with the spirit. Man is a spiritual being. He shares the potency of his ancestors, i.e., if he is potent biologically, his nonbiological or spiritual life is also potent. Hansberry confirmed the spiritual health of the family; however, her primary failing was conceiving the Younger family in sociological terms, which leave the problems of their existence in a frozen state, locked into categorical imperatives. By no means does this suggest that she lacks a complete understanding of the family's oppression. It would seem, rather, that she acted on an impulse derived from her native sensibility to urge, in fact, Nommo the situation toward some humane, harmonious conclusion. It is highly improbable that a woman of her intelligence could have construed the inappropriate happy ending of the play as being meaningful unless it was in response to her deep-seated desire to accomplish what reality could not achieve. Even Hansberry could not have been so naive as to think that the modality of white oppression could be broken because of a black family's integration into a white neighborhood.

Walter Becomes a Man When He Learns to Be Like His Father

William Cook

William Cook is the Israel Evans Professor Emeritus of Oratory and Belles Lettres at Dartmouth College.

In the following selection, Cook asserts that while the head of the Younger household may seem to be Lena, in reality she takes her cues from what her deceased husband, Walter Senior, would have wished for the family. It is his value system that guides Mama Lena in her dealings with her children, rather than a wish to control them absolutely as the black matriarch stereotype would have readers believe. According to Cook, Walter achieves manhood at the play's conclusion when he rejects the superficial values of streetwise role models such as Willy Harris and lets his mother guide him toward adopting the combination of religious and secular moral values that were his father's.

Lena Younger, materfamilias [female head of the house-hold] of Lorraine Hansberry's *A Raisin in the Sun*, has become something of an archetype of the Black matriarch—that powerful and commanding figure who inaugurates and imposes the life-style which she considers appropriate for the world she sees. A careful consideration of the play, however, might point to another function for Hansberry's mother. Since the play opens after the death of the father, it is easy to dismiss his role as dictator of values and at the same time to exaggerate the control which Lena exercises. Lena Younger's function in the play is not so much to create values and to

William Cook, "Mom, Dad and God: Values in Black Theater," in *The Theater of Black Americans*, vol. 1, edited by Errol Hill, Upper Saddle River, NJ: Prentice-Hall, 1980, pp. 170–173. Copyright © 1980 Prentice-Hall, Inc. All rights reserved. Used by permission of Prentice-Hall/A Division of Simon & Schuster, Upper Saddle River, NJ.

impose her will on her children as it is to interpret for them Walter Senior's values and to mold them into the kind of people he would have them be. When she speaks of values, she refers not to values that are hers alone, but rather to values which she shared with her husband. This is apparent in her response to Walter Lee's ambitions and his subsequent disenchantment. Having faced defeat, he voices a philosophy of bitterness that is opposed to the life-view which Lena and her husband espoused. Walter Lee releases in his conversation with Murchison all the bile that has been building up inside him:

> And you—ain't you bitter, man? Ain't you just about had it yet? Don't you see no stars gleaming that you can't reach out and grab? . . . Bitter? Man I'm a volcano. Bitter?

Later he voices this same dark pessimism in response to his sister's criticism of him:

> There ain't no causes—there ain't nothing but taking in this world, and he who takes the most is smartest—and it don't make a damn bit of difference how.

Walter Senior as the Source of Values

In countering this view with her attitude toward life, it is significant to note that Lena sees Walter Senior and not herself as the source and example of these values:

> Oh Big Walter, is this the harvest of our days?

The notion that values clarification for the family is a joint effort of the father and mother is clear in the following exchange with her daughter:

> *Beneatha.* Wasn't it you who taught me to despise any man who would do that. Do what he's going to do?
>
> *Mama.* Yes—I taught you that. Me and your Daddy. I taught you something else, too. . . . I thought I taught you to love

him. There is always something left to love.... When do you think is the time to love somebody the most; when they done good and made things easy for everybody? Well then, you ain't through learning—because that ain't the time at all. It's when he's at his lowest and can't believe in himself cause the world done whipped him so.

That these are not empty words is apparent in Lena's conduct, for she has seen her husband and now her son reach this "low ground of sorrow" and yet has not given way to bitterness or scorn. Qualities that were so evident in her life with her husband are the ones she attempts to instill in her children for, to her, they are enduring values; as relevant to the experience of Beneatha and Walter, Jr.—symbols of the new generation—as they were to her husband and her. Big Walter laid the foundations for this view of life when he sacrificed for his family, accepted defeat without becoming bitter or self-destructive, assumed responsibility for the welfare of his family and placed that welfare and love above any personal material gain he might have realized.

Father as Role Model

At the close of Act I, Lena states directly for the first time the proper direction for her son: he is to be the man his father was. Her words are those of a loving mother who wants her son to become a man in the fullest sense of that term. They are hardly the words of a woman desiring to control and castrate him:

> I waiting to hear how you be your father's son. Be the man he was.... And I'm waiting to hear you talk like him and say we a people who give children life, not who destroys them—I'm waiting to see you stand up and look like your daddy and say we done give up one baby to poverty and that we ain't going to give up nary another one.... I'm waiting.

Walter, blinded by the materialistic values of the society in which he lives and deaf to anything but the voices that speak to him of his own success in the "corporate" world, cannot be touched by such a plea or inspired by such an example. He does not respond. "You're a disgrace to your father's memory." By invoking the father's memory Lena has tried to guide her son in the way of manhood and has failed to do so.

In the final act of the play, however, she repeats this attempt with greater success. Walter has grown; he's "come into his manhood." When Walter faces Lindner in the closing scene of the play, Lena challenges his decision to humble himself by placing his son before him, thus forcing Walter to see himself as heir to a proud and strong sense of family. He is the son of his father and can he now act in such a way that he disgraces his heritage? Walter, finally remembering and honoring this heritage, responds not as he has had planned but as a man dedicated to continuing the work his father began:

> This is my son, who makes the sixth generation of our family in this country. . . . We have decided to move into our house because my father—he earned it.

Achieving Manhood

Walter comes into his manhood when he chooses his father's values and rejects the corrupted standards which he has learned from the Murchisons and Willy Harrises of the world. He matures when he decides that whether it profit him or no, he will live according to those values and not submit to the grab-what-you-can mentality of his world.

It is not surprising to any student of Black drama that the church or, perhaps more accurately, religion, plays a role in shaping the values for which Lena Younger is the medium. Her religion is a source of strength when she feels that she lacks the power to deal with life. Her prayer at the end of Act II is not an empty ritual but rather a plea for strength to resist the bitterness and despair that threaten to destroy her and her family:

> Oh God ... Look down here—and show me the strength. Strength. ... Strength!

Any careful reader and especially any actress interested in understanding how to play these lines will realize that the repetition of the last word is not mere restatement. By the third utterance we should see a woman who has been strengthened, who has triumphed over the darkness that has engulfed her for so many years.

Act I closes with the evocation of the father as symbol of pride and familial love; Act II closes with the evocation of God as a source of strength and endurance. We have here the twin springs from which Lena draws her sustenance: her husband's way of life and her religious faith. For this reason, the closing moments of Act III are very telling. When Walter finally taps the well of pride and power that is his father's memory, when he becomes the man his father was, Lena is described as having "her eyes closed ... rocking back and forth as though she were in church, with her head nodding the amen Yes." The transformation of the boy Walter into the man is complete, the restoration of the father as source of pride is accomplished, the integration of religious values with secular concerns has triumphed and Lena, high priestess and exegete [one who interprets holy scripture], can say amen and rest.

Hansberry's Drama Rejects the Stereotype of the Emasculating Woman

Sharon Friedman

Sharon Friedman is an associate professor in the Gallatin School of Individualized Study at New York University. She is the editor of the book Feminist Theatrical Revisions of Classic Works.

Lorraine Hansberry's feminist attitude is easy to overlook in A Raisin in the Sun, *but in the following selection, Friedman observes that in both this play and her later, unfinished slave drama,* The Drinking Gourd, *Hansberry espouses feminist themes. Friedman explains that it is common to view Lena Younger as Walter's chief antagonist in his quest for a better life, but Walter comes to realize that it is societal oppression and not the women in his life who are impeding him. In* The Drinking Gourd, *Friedman points out, Hansberry shatters the image of the black Mammy, as the play's matriarch, Rissa, plays an active role in raising determined, rebellious sons. In the author's view, the actions of Hansberry's mothers refute the stereotypes that label black women as either passive or emasculating.*

In portraying ... formidable though not demoniac women, Lorraine Hansberry clearly shows that the perception of women's emasculating behavior is itself rooted in patriarchal values. One of the least recognized aspects of Hansberry's plays are the feminist concerns woven into her exploration of racial and economic oppression, and the struggle against political and human alienation. Writing on the eve of the recent feminist resurgence, Hansberry anticipates in her characterizations of strong and admirable black women the black

Sharon Friedman, "Feminism as Theme in Twentieth-Century American Women's Drama," *American Studies,* vol. 25, no. 1, 1984, pp. 84–86. Reproduced by permission.

feminists of the '60s and '70s who have repudiated attacks upon black women, particularly mothers, as castrating and conservative—a restraining force upon rebellion. Hansberry's mothers are at times difficult, but they are also supportive and often revolutionary.

Hansberry as Feminist

In an article titled "This Complex of Womanhood," Hansberry's most direct feminist statement, she brings attention to the realities underlying stereotypical images of black women:

> ... On the one hand ... she is saluted as a monument of endurance and fortitude, and in whose bosom all comforts reside ... and, at the same time, another legend of the Negro woman describes the most ... deprecating creature ever placed on earth to plague ... the male. She is seen as an over-practical, unreasonable source of the destruction of all vision and totally lacking a sense of the proper "place" of womanhood.

> Either image taken alone is romance; put together they embrace some truths and present the complex of womanhood which ... now awakens to find itself inextricably ... bound to the world's most insurgent elements.... [i]n the United States, a seamstress refuses one day, simply refuses, to move from her chosen place on a bus while an equally remarkable sister of hers ushers children past bayonets in Little Rock. It is indeed a single march, a unified destiny, and the prize is the future.... In behalf of an ailing world which surely needs our defiance, may we, as Negroes or *women* never accept the notion of "our place."

In *A Raisin in the Sun* (1959), Hansberry's drama about a family anxious to leave their roach-infested apartment on Chicago's Southside, she portrays such a traditional and at the same time forward-looking woman in the character of Lena Younger. Lena, or Mama, as she is called, comes into conflict with her son Walter about the means for attaining a better life for their family—his sister, wife and child. The play employs a device, a $10,000 insurance policy that comes to Lena after her husband's death. Lena as well as the other women want to buy a house and move the family out of the ghetto. She also plans to set money aside for her daughter's medical education. But Walter, pained by his life as a chauffeur and by his inability to provide for his family, wants to invest in a liquor store, and ultimately loses a large sum in pursuit of quick money.

Walter eventually attains a sense of self-realization, not by forfeiting his dreams and acquiescing to the women's demands, nor by moving into a white neighborhood, but rather by resisting the attempts of the white community to exclude him by buying him off. Moreover, Walter's self-awareness is achieved through transferring the target of his resentment from black women to those who have the power to control his fate.

Rejecting the Emasculating Black Woman Stereotype

Early in the play, Walter castigates black women (his wife Ruth in particular) for not "building their men up and making 'em feel like they somebody. Like they can do something. . . ." Because black women exert a profound influence on family decisions, they are seen to be a further assault on his manhood. Walter perceives their strength as a source of his weakness.

Hansberry rejects the idea that black women "emasculate" black men, as well as the notion that emasculation is the cause of black social and economic inferiority. *A Raisin in the Sun* debunks these myths by portraying the real causes of frustration and self-hatred: the race prejudice and economic exploitation which oppress black men and women alike, and which strain their personal relations.

Hansberry's feminism is implicit in her dramatization of these personal relations within the domestic sphere. The condition of women forced to work at subsistence wages and relegated to domestic labor is epitomized by Hansberry in her portrayal of the black domestic who must clean the kitchens of white women as well as her own. At the same time, she is expected to bolster the male ego which has been deflated by racism and poverty. Because it is women who are charged with the responsibility of raising children and maintaining the home even under the most adverse conditions, it is not surprising that Hansberry portrays the women in this play as particularly anxious to acquire a better home. Yet because of their urgency to move the family out of the ghetto, they are vulnerable to Walter's accusations (shared by some critics) of "not thinking big enough" and of frustrating men's ambitions. Hansberry's answer is that the ghetto kills not only the dreams to which Mama clings, but the bodies of the children Ruth must feed or abort.

Shattering the Black Mammy Image

It is perhaps easy to misperceive Lena Younger as an example of the courageous but inhibiting black mother image, which at least one critic has observed in contemporary black drama. However, Rissa, in [Hansberry's play] *The Drinking Gourd* (1960), a jolting variation of the prototypical black Mammy in the Slave South, shatters this image for good. Rissa turns her back on the dying master, Hiram Sweet, who had for years given her a privileged position among the slaves, when she realizes that he is responsible, even though indirectly, for blinding her son—his punishment for learning to react. In the last scene of the play, Rissa is shown giving Hiram's gun to the blind Hannibal whom she helps to escape. Thus, she aids insurgency while toppling the myth of the forgiving Mammy. In [Hansberry's husband] Robert Nemiroff's words, Rissa "literally reverses the image."

Lena (Claudia McNeil) defies gender stereotypes as the strong-willed mother of Walter (Sidney Poitier) in Daniel Petrie's film version of A Raisin in the Sun. *AP Images.*

At first glance, Rissa appears to restrain her son by making him as comfortable as possible in his slave role. She connives to secure him a position in the main house, and reminds him that, as a slave owner, Hiram Sweet is better than most. However, it is important to note the details which Hansberry has carefully worked into her drama to signify that Hannibal has inherited his spirit of rebellion from his mother, and that she is more an accomplice than an obstacle. When he informs his mother that he has learned to read, she is overcome with a wonder and joy that are rapidly "transformed to stark fear" for his life. Hannibal expects her joy, even when he is disappointed by her fear, for he knows that Rissa possesses the spirit of resistance which eventually leads her to steal Hiram's gun. Indeed, he has heard the songs of insurgency late at night in his mother's cabin, a center of domestic life for the slave community. It is not a mere coincidence that Rissa has "birthed" two sons determined to follow the Drinking Gourd (an old slave metaphor for the Big Dipper which points to the North Star, the symbol and beacon of freedom for runaway slaves), for in subtle ways she had woven this spirit into the fabric of their daily lives.

Hansberry's mothers, Lena and Rissa, repudiate the negative images of black women as passive and/or destructive. Indeed, the playwright has created women who contribute not only to the survival of their families and communities, but also to the active resistance often necessary to that survival.

A Raisin in the Sun Is Dominated by Women

Anita Singh

Anita Singh is a lecturer in the Department of English at Banaras Hindu University in India.

In this selection, Singh writes that the struggle to define women's role in the theater has been ongoing for twenty-five hundred years and shows no signs of being resolved. A Raisin in the Sun is a play that shows a double consciousness: the struggle of the American woman as well as the black woman. According to Singh, the play is about the aspirations and anxieties of its three main women, each of whom has the strength necessary to meet the challenges of the contemporary world. The play dramatizes the struggle of all women who are appalled by present conditions and seek a new, better world, Singh avers.

As the dreamer is the author of the dreams, so, too, it is the polis or community that makes the stories it tells in its drama. The struggle to define women's proper place in the theatre has been going on for at least 2,500 years and shows no signs, as we stand on this new millennium, of being resolved.

Among the most perturbing of such theatre are those by black American Women playwrights. For them there is a complicated double consciousness in which they see the world as an American Woman and a black woman. From the beginnings of theatre by black women playwrights to the present, these women's dramas have tended to create stage worlds in which diverse voices and world-views collide, polyphony

Anita Singh, "Look Back in Gender: Lorraine Hansberry's *A Raisin in the Sun*," in *Studies in Women Writers in English*, edited by Mohit K. Ray and Rama Kundu, New Delhi: Atlantic, 2005, pp. 31–35. Copyright © Atlantic Publishers and Distributors 2005. Reproduced by permission.

[many voices] is asserted and sometimes celebrated and different signifying systems of dance, music and visual imagery are aggressively utilized.

A Milestone in Black Women's Drama

The black, long either a subject of indifference or, at best the concern of self-conscious white writer, began to speak for himself/herself with greater force from the early twentieth century. Lorraine Hansberry's *A Raisin in the Sun* (1959) was a milestone in black women's drama. It was the first play written by a black woman to be produced on Broadway, and the first play by a black woman to win New York Drama Critics Circle Award. The play, a domestic comedy with overtones of emotion, some close to soap opera, is out of ordinary in its warm, human way with blacks whose problems, not unlike those of families everywhere, loom so much larger simply because their skins were dark. Written in the political and cultural ambience of the Integrationist Movement, it is a social protest play intended to persuade white people that black people are not only good at heart but sufficiently like whites in their values and cultural practices for whites to allow blacks to be their neighbours. The title of the play, taken from Langston Hughes's verse,

> What happens to a dream deferred?
>
> Does it dry up
>
> Like a raisin in the sun?
>
> Or fester like a sore—
>
> And then run?
>
> Does it stink like rotten meat:
>
> Or crust and sugar over—
>
> Like a syrupy sweet?
>
> May be it just sags
>
> Like a heavy load.

Or does it explode?

is suggestive of the explosive quality of the dreams nurtured by the Younger family—Walter, Mama, Ruth and Beneatha.

The action of the play is set in Chicago's Southside, sometime between World War II and the present. The play is in three acts.

The characters are drawn from plain working class. Walter has worked as a chauffeur most of his life, his wife Ruth did domestic work in people's kitchen, so did his mother. Travis, Walter and Ruth's son, belongs to the sixth generation of their family in America.

Dramas Dominated by Women

Hansberry's dramas are dominated by women. Motherhood is the centre of appeal; the play is a representation of what it means to love as a mother and to be a black American woman. The three female characters in the play are strongly portrayed. Mama, Mrs Lena Younger, is a woman in her early sixties, full bodied and strong. Being a woman who had adjusted to many things in life and overcome many more, her face is full of strength. Ruth, about thirty, must have been a pretty girl but when the play starts, disappointment has already begun to hang in her face. Beneatha is about twenty, as slim and intense as her brother Walter. She is not as pretty as her sister-in-law, Ruth, but her lean, almost intellectual face has a handsomeness of its own.

The central interest of the play hinges on a cheque which Mama is expecting from her husband's insurance money. She takes a firm decision, negating her son Walter's dream of setting up a liquor shop.

> Mama: (Quietly) I don't low no yellin' in this house, Walter Lee, and you know it—And there ain't going to be no investing in no liquor stores. I don't aim to have to speak on that again.

Thus explicitly stating who's at the helm of affairs at home.

The play articulates the anxieties and aspirations of three black women, projected by mama (Mrs. Lena Younger), who has lived through difficult times: "In my time we was worried about not being lynched and getting to the north if we could and how to stay alive and still have a pinch of dignity too." She cherishes a dream of owning a house:

A nice house. Three bedrooms, nice big one for you and Ruth [...]. And a little yard with a patch of dirt where I could maybe get to grow me a few flowers [...]. And a nice big basement.

Ruth also shares Mama's dream of owning a nice house.

Beneatha, the youngest of the three is completely disillusioned with the Integrationist principles, She declares:

I hate assimilationist Negroes [...]. It means someone who is willing to give up his own culture and submerge himself completely in the dominant, and in this case, oppressive culture.

She is infuriated when George Murchison, her boyfriend, tells her that "your heritage is nothing but a bunch of raggedly assed spirituals and some grasshuts." She defiantly retorts: "See there [...] you are standing there in your splendid ignorance talking about people who were the first to smelt iron on the face of the earth. The Ashanti were performing surgical operations when the English were still tattooing themselves with blue dragons."

Thus she determinedly demonstrates the supremacy of the black civilization. She too has a dream, a dream of becoming a doctor:

I always thought it was one concrete thing in the world that a human being could do. Fix up the sick, you know—and make them whole again. This was truly being God.

Among those troublesome, marginalized issues, is the pregnancy of Ruth. She finds no joy in the prospect of bringing another child into the grim and potentially explosive world, [and] makes plans for an abortion. When Ruth's husband Walter expresses his disbelief about Ruth trying to get rid of the child, Mama knowingly says: "When the world gets ugly enough—a woman will do anything for her family. The part that's already living." However, she does not have an abortion in the end.

Suffering, Endurance, and Dreams

The play is powerfully sustained by the suffering, endurance and dreams of these three women. Mama (Mrs Lena Younger), in a bid to retrieve some of the lost happiness of the Younger family, goes out and buys a house from her husband's insurance money. Justifying the need for a house, she tells her son Walter:

> Son—you—you understand what I done, don't you? I—I just seen my family falling apart today [...] just falling to pieces in front of my eyes [...]. We couldn't of gone on like we were today. We were going backwards stead of forwards— talking bout killing babies and wishing each other was dead [...] when it gets like that in life you just got to do something different, push on out and do something bigger.

But when she realizes that she has butchered up her son's dream, she says: "There ain't nothing worth holding on to, money, dreams, nothing else—if it means—if it means its going to destroy my boy." For Ruth the purchase of the house is like a dream come true; she raises both her arms classically and makes an attempt to pacify, her husband: "please, honey let me be glad [...] you be glad too [...] oh, Walter, a home [...] a home."

The family witnesses disillusionment of their cherished dreams. Walter's dream of a liquor shop, Beneatha's of becoming a doctor goes to dust when Walter messes up the money by foolishly trusting the unscrupulous Willy with his money.

Women Creating a New World

The euphoria of the new house is also shattered, one week later when the Younger family receives a caller, Mr. Karl Linder, a representative of the Clybourne Park Improvement Association, who had come in a bid to buy the house from the family at financial gain to the family, in order to restrain the coloured family from occupying a house in a white community. When Mama wants to know if they were threatened, Beneatha's bitterness spills out: "oh-Mama—They don't do it like that any more, he talked Brotherhood. He said everybody ought to learn how to sit down and hate each other with good Christian fellowship." In the play's conclusion, Walter regains his dignity by informing the white man that the Youngers have changed their minds and will move into their house in the white neighbourhood. In spite of all the reverses of fate, Ruth has tenaciously clung to her dream of moving out and with an urgency and desperation makes a fierce declaration at the end of play:

> I'll strap my baby on my back if I have to and scrub all the floors in America and wash all the sheets in America if I have to—but we got to move, we got to get out of here. "Let's GET THE HELL OUT OF HERE!"

This landmark of black women's drama presents a vision of a theatre and a world informed by what [British media critic] Raymond Williams has called "a new tragic consciousness." This play represents the position of all those who, appalled by the present, are for this reason firmly committed to a different future: to the struggle against suffering learned in suffering: a total exposure which is also a total involvement. To fulfil this vision black women's dramas re-create world's past and present in terms of a redefined notion of heritage and inspire our conviction that things could, indeed, be different.

Hansberry's Play Depicts Strong-Willed Women Who Refuse to Be Marginalized

Sally Burke

Sally Burke is professor emerita of English and Women's studies at the University of Rhode Island.

In the following selection, Burke writes that Lorraine Hansberry is a herald of second-wave feminism, the women's movement that arose in the 1960s and 1970s. Her writing clearly displays her feminist philosophy, and A Raisin in the Sun *is no exception. Burke asserts that Lena, Ruth, and Beneatha are strong, three-dimensional characters who are complex enough to resist easy stereotypes. In their depictions Hansberry refutes the notion that women are inferior to men. Even the often-sexist Walter Lee acknowledges their strength and the validity of their dreams in his speech to Lindner near the end of the play.*

As a herald of the second wave of the women's movement, Lorraine Hansberry lived and wrote a feminism not widely recognized in her lifetime and one inseparable from her identity as an African American. In an unpublished essay on [French feminist writer] Simone de Beauvoir, she states her position:

> Woman, like the Negro, like the Jew, like colonial peoples, even in ignorance, *is incapable of accepting the role with harmony*. This is because it is an unnatural role. . . . The station of woman is hardly one that she would assume by choice, any more than men would. It must necessarily be imposed on her—by force. . . . A status not freely chosen or entered

into by an individual or group is necessarily one of oppression and the oppressed are by their nature . . . forever in ferment and agitation against their condition and what they understand to be their oppressors. If not by overt rebellion or revolution, then in the thousand and one ways they will devise with and without consciousness to alter their condition.

Hansberry and the Women's Movement

Also cognizant of class issues, Hansberry warned against "an illusion . . . that our country is made up of one huge sprawling middle class whose problems, valid though they are as subject matter, are considered to represent the problems of the entire nation and whose values are thought to be not only the values of the nation but, significantly enough, of the whole world!"

Hansberry spoke as she wrote; in an interview published posthumously in the November 1984 *American Theatre* magazine, she anticipated the resurgence of the women's movement, noting, "Obviously the most oppressed group of any oppressed group will be its women, who are twice oppressed. So I should imagine that they react accordingly: As oppression makes people more militant, women become *twice* militant, because they are twice oppressed." Hansberry located this oppression in the social construct of "woman." In a letter to a friend, she commented on its use in *After the Fall*. Finding [*After the Fall*'s author] Arthur Miller "incapable of indicting the social order" that destroyed [actress, sex symbol, and Miller's wife] Marilyn Monroe, Hansberry writes, "the concept of 'woman' which fashioned, warped and destroyed a human being such as Marilyn Monroe (or 'Audrey Smith' or 'Jean West' or 'Lucy Jones')—*daily* IS HIDEOUSLY WRONG—and she, *in her repudiation of it*, in trying tragically to RISE ABOVE it by killing herself is (in the Shakespearean sense)—right. Such a life as hers was an affront to *her humanity*."

Women are central to Hansberry's dramas, in which [according to *Notable Women in American Theatre*] her "portrayals of women challenged prevailing stage stereotypes of both black and white females and introduced feminist issues to the stage in compelling terms." These dramatic characters joined the real women who marched in the parade she described in the September 1963 edition of *Ebony* magazine: "It is indeed a single march, a unified destiny and the prize is the future. . . . Above all, in behalf of an ailing world which sorely needs our defiance, may we as Negroes or women never accept the notion of—'our place.'" In her first and most successful drama, Hansberry presents in Lena, Ruth, and Beneatha Younger women who refuse to be relegated to "their place."

Black and Feminist Consciousness

A Raisin in the Sun enjoyed a run of 538 performances on Broadway, won a special award for its film version at the Cannes Film Festival in 1961, and was televised by the Public Broadcasting System's *American Playhouse* in 1989 in a version that restored most of the cuts made for various reasons in the Broadway original. When the New York Drama Critics Circle recognized her work over competition from [American playwright Eugene] O'Neill's *A Touch of the Poet* and [American playwright Tennessee] Williams's *Sweet Bird of Youth*, Hansberry became the first black, the fifth woman, and the youngest American to win its award for best play. Reviews were enthusiastic. In the 28 March 1959 *New York Times*, Brooks Atkinson found the play to be "honest" and added, "*A Raisin In The Sun* has vigor as well as veracity and is likely to destroy the complacency of any one who sees it." [American theater director and drama critic] Harold Clurman, in the 4 April 1959 issue of the *Nation*, described it as "an honestly felt response to a situation that has been lived through, clearly understood, and therefore simply and impressively stated." On 22 March 1959 the *New York Herald Tribune*'s Walter Kerr discerned the social and political qualities in the play, commenting that the playwright "reads the precise temperature of a race at that time in its history when it cannot retreat and cannot quite find the way to move forward. The mood is forty-nine parts anger and forty-nine parts control, with a very narrow escape hatch for the steam these abrasive contraries build up. Three generations stand poised, and crowded, on a detonation cap."

[Author Sharon] Friedman notes a connection between [American playwright Lillian] Hellman and Hansberry, declaring that, like Hellman, "Hansberry is [a] playwright whose awareness of a feminist perspective, particularly as it illuminates the experience of black women, is demonstrated in relation to social issues." Among these social issues is one that was of utmost importance to the women playwrights of the Harlem Renaissance: lynching. Like [American playwrights Angelina Weld] Grimké, [Georgia Douglas] Johnson, and [Mary P.] Burrill, Hansberry reminds her audience of the perils of instant white "justice," as Lena Younger recalls her not-so-distant past: "In my time we was worried about not being lynched and getting to the North if we could and how to stay alive and still have a pinch of dignity." Even as Hansberry recalled the past, she pointed toward the factors fueling the coming revolutions in black and feminist consciousness, incorporating into the play such issues as the link between Africa and African Americans, racism, threats to the black family's survival, assimilation, the generation gap, abortion, feminism, and male/female relationships. The effect on black audiences was electric. [African American novelist] James Baldwin wrote, "I had never in my life seen so many black people in the theater. And the reason was that never before, in the entire history of the American theater, has so much truth of black people's lives been seen on the stage."

Raisin's Plot

The plot focuses on the Younger family, three generations crowded into a kitchenette apartment on the Southside of Chicago, and on the dreams engendered in each member by a $10,000 life insurance settlement. Walter Lee, a chauffeur, hopes to become part-owner of a liquor store; his sister Beneatha wants help with medical school tuition, while Lena, Walter's mother, and Ruth, his wife, dream of escaping the ghetto by buying a home where there is room for all, fresh air, and sunlight. After making a down payment on a house in a white neighborhood, Lena, realizing Walter's need to control his own life, gives him the remaining $6,500. Although she tells him to put half in the bank for Beneatha's education, Walter naively entrusts all the money to his dishonest partner, who flees with the cash. In a desperate effort to atone for his error, Walter decides to accept the previously rejected offer of the white neighborhood's representative to buy out the family. As he rehearses his Uncle Tom act for Mama, she tells him: "Son—I come from five generations of people who was slaves and sharecroppers—but ain't nobody in my family never let nobody pay 'em no money that was a way of telling us we wasn't fit to walk the earth. We ain't never been that poor. . . . We ain't never been that—dead inside." She insists that his 10-year-old son witness the sellout. His mother's steel enters Walter's spine and, instead of accepting the bribe, he informs Lindner that the family will, indeed, be moving to Clybourne Park. As the play ends, the family members pack their worn furniture and deferred dreams and prepare to face the threats, fears, and possible violence awaiting them in their new home.

Lena Younger Motivated by Love

Although Walter acts as spokesman, it is the women in the family who move him beyond his devotion to the material aspect of the American Dream and beyond the sexism that allows him to view himself as castrated by the women in his family rather than by racism and materialism. Mama, described as possessing "the noble bearing of the women of the Hereroes of Southwest Africa" and sometimes deferentially addressed as "Miss Lena" by her daughter-in-law, Ruth, appears at first to be the stereotypical matriarch. She has worked as a domestic, sees marriage as a woman's role and destiny, claims that because her grandson is "a little boy [he] ain't supposed to know 'bout housekeeping," objects to the idea of selling liquor, and clings to a conservative Christianity. Her dream, since marrying Big Walter, has been to escape the "rat trap" of the ghetto, where her grandson literally finds it sport to watch the janitor corner and kill a rat. Now she plans to take the life insurance settlement and fulfill that dream, not only for herself but also for her family, a family breaking apart as Walter berates Ruth for failing to support his dreams and quarrels with Beneatha over her aspiration to become a doctor. Seeing her children setting at each other like rats in a trap, Mama puts a down payment on a house where "there's a whole lot of sunlight."

Mama does not act arbitrarily but only for what she considers the good of her well-loved family; she does not wish to control her children and her grandson for the sake of maintaining power, but only to continue to provide growth and opportunity for them. That she, along with her husband, had done so in the past is evident when she points out to Walter Lee, "You ain't satisfied or proud of nothing we done. I mean that you had a home; that we kept you out of trouble till you was grown; that you don't have to ride to work on the back of nobody's streetcar." Here Mama becomes the embodiment of consciousness raising, the representative of the Civil Rights movement as it was also embodied in the real-life heroics of another determined black woman, Rosa Parks.

On the other hand, Mama is not blind to Walter's needs. She makes him trustee of the remainder of the insurance money, and even when he loses it to his crooked putative

Lorraine Hansberry is heralded as a second-wave feminist for her powerful, complex female characters, such as Lena, Beneatha, and Ruth, played by Phylicia Rashad, Sanaa Lathan, and Audra McDonald respectively. The actresses are shown here in the 2008 television adaption of A Raisin in the Sun. *Mario Anzuoni/Reuters/Landov.*

partner, continues to love him, because "the time to love somebody the most ... [is] when he's at his lowest and can't believe in hisself 'cause the world done whipped him so!" She responds to Lindner's appeal that she urge her son not to insist on moving by making Walter's status as new head of the household official: "My son said we was going to move and there ain't nothing left for me to say."

Beneatha Rejects Subservience

While Lena's deference to her son, reminiscent of [American playwright Rachel] Crothers's Rhy McChesney [in the play *The Three of Us*] ceding her self-determination to her brother Clem to make a man of him, is appropriate to a woman of Lena's generation, Walter's sister, Beneatha, makes no concessions as she resists pressures from family and suitors to surrender her dreams. As her mother refuses to accept a rat-infested, cockroach-ridden ghetto as her place, Beneatha refuses to accept the subservient position often seen as "natural" for women. From childhood she has dreamed of being a doctor, and her brother's telling her to "go be a nurse like other women—or just get married and be quiet" only strengthens her determination. Though two attractive young men pursue her, Beneatha will not be pushed into accommodating their patriarchal ideas of what she should be. The wealthy African American assimilationist George Murchison values her for her good looks and tells her, "You're a nice looking girl . . . all over. That's all you need, honey, forget the atmosphere. . . . I don't go out with you to discuss the nature of 'quiet desperation' or to hear all about your thoughts." Joseph Asagai, a Nigerian, also vies for Beneatha's affection. Asagai's position is ambiguous; he sometimes laughs at Bennie and answers her protest about his inability to understand "that there is more than one kind of feeling which can exist between a man and a woman" by insisting that "[b]etween a man and a woman there need be only one kind of feeling" and that "[f]or a woman it should be enough." Yet he counterpoises this sexism with a refusal to allow her to rationalize surrendering her dream merely because Walter has lost the money. He answers her metaphysical question about where we all are going and why we all are bothering by reminding her of what she already knows. His "I live the answer" speech repeats the feminist philosophy Hansberry stated: "Man is unique in the universe, the only creature who has in fact power to transform the universe. Therefore, it [does] not seem unthinkable to me that man might just do what the apes never will—*impose* the reason for life on life." Beneatha finds Asagai's response and the man himself attractive, but insists on taking time to think, thus remaining consistent with Hansberry's portrayal of her as a young woman who will control her own destiny. Here Hansberry, like Hellman, invests hope for the future in the rising generation.

Ruth as Midpoint

Ruth occupies a midpoint between Mama and Beneatha. Like Lena, Ruth works as a domestic and suffers the indignity of employers who refer to her as "my girl." She is a loyal wife to Walter, doing his bidding by speaking to Lena about investing in the liquor store. Like her mother-in-law, Ruth sees marriage as woman's destiny and is not above encouraging Beneatha to marry George Murchison because of his money. Yet Ruth is not altogether trapped in thinking dictated by the patriarchy. Faced with the prospect of bringing another child into the already overcrowded Younger apartment, Ruth, without consulting anyone, reluctantly makes a down payment on an abortion. Much as she wants her child, Ruth also knows that she has the right to control her body. Ultimately, she is spared from taking what she sees as this painful step; when Lena buys the house, Ruth expresses her joy at being able to continue her pregnancy by shouting "PRAISE GOD!" When Walter loses the money, Ruth promises Mama, "I'll work twenty hours a day in all the kitchens in Chicago . . . I'll strap my baby on my back if I have to and scrub all the floors in America." Thus she expresses both her own agency and the urgency of the family's need to leave the ghetto.

Acknowledging Three Strong Women

All three women, while nurturing different dreams, exhibit strength of spirit, will, and mind. Through them, Hansberry refutes the view of women as lesser beings, properly subject to the will of men.

And once Walter recognizes the nature of his true legacy, he pays homage to these remarkable yet ordinary women. Initially, Walter perceives the insurance money as his inheritance; through the proposed investment in the liquor store, he dreams of multiplying this $10,000 into a sum that will buy Chryslers and Cadillacs, a home complete with gardener, and an education at one of "the great schools in America" for his son. The insurance money represents to Walter a piece of the materialistic American Dream. Only after the money is lost does Walter come into his true legacy: the promise of America that lies in freedom, the right of self determination, and the right to live where one chooses. This legacy, too, has been too long delayed; racism leads whites to attempt to buy the blacks' freedom and, failing that, to intimidate them through fear. When he spurns Lindner's offer, Walter has learned that, in fact, money can be squandered or lost to a cheat, but, though blacks are forced to fight for it, the truly valuable legacy—freedom—remains. Here Hansberry asserts humankind's right to a decent home and a comfortable standard of living while she rejects the blatant materialism that drove Walter's earlier vision. Freed of that distorted dream, Walter acknowledges to Lindner not only the flesh of the father that purchased the $10,000 dream but also his wife and his mother, who do "domestic work in people's kitchens," and his "sister [who's] going to be a doctor," the women who live the more precious dream.

Beneatha Fights Male Chauvinism as Well as Her Own Flaws

Steven R. Carter

Steven R. Carter has taught at the University of North Carolina, the University of Puerto Rico, and, currently, at Salem State College in Massachusetts. He is the author of numerous articles on Lorraine Hansberry, as well as of the book Hansberry's Drama: Commitment amid Complexity.

In this essay Carter examines Lorraine Hansberry's characterization of Beneatha, who must deal with the male chauvinism of her brother as well as of her two suitors, George Murchison and Joseph Asagai. Both Murchison and Asagai are flawed characters who nevertheless demonstrate potential—particularly Asagai, who is willing to take Beneatha's career goals seriously. Carter states that, in spite of the racism and sexism Beneatha contends with, Beneatha is similar to Walter. Both brother and sister fight for their dreams, and both display selfishness that mars them as characters. In Carter's view, Beneatha's extravagant spending on her hobbies, such as horseback-riding, is particularly troubling in light of the fifty cents denied to Ruth's son, and this detail damages Hansberry's play as a whole.

L ike Walter, both of Beneatha's suitors display male chauvinism, although in varying degrees. Murchison, for example, regards Beneatha's desire to be a doctor as laughable, and when she tries to talk to him seriously, he advises her: "I want you to cut it out, see—The moody stuff, I mean. I don't like it. You're a nice-looking girl . . . all over. That's all you

Steven R. Carter, *Hansberry's Drama: Commitment amid Complexity*, Champaign, IL: University of Illinois Press, 1991, pp. 58–63. Copyright © 1991 by the Board of Trustees of the University of Illinois. Reproduced by permission of the University of Illinois Press.

need, honey, forget the atmosphere. Guys aren't going to go for the atmosphere—they're going to go for what they see. Be glad for that".

Not surprisingly, Beneatha dismisses him as a fool.

Flaws and Potential

Her other suitor, Asagai, cannot be so easily dismissed, however. His beguiling mixture of idealism and sophistication, his seeming role as spokesperson for Hansberry's political and philosophical views, his professed dedication to the liberation of his country from colonialism and professed willingness to die for it all lend him the aura of a romantic hero. Nevertheless, he is capable of such insensitive comments as "between a man and a woman there need be only one kind of feeling" and "for a woman [love] should be enough." These remarks imply that in spite of all his revolutionary attitudes he is, in this area, a traditional—and fallible—male. (Hansberry's clear-sighted vision saw the flaws and potential for change in everyone.) Unlike Murchison, though, he is willing to listen to Beneatha and take her career goals seriously, thus enabling their relationship to grow and leaving open the possibility that he may eventually free himself of his remaining chauvinism.

In contrast to Asagai, George Murchison remains almost as shackled to other forms of folly as he is to male chauvinism. Through him, Hansberry satirizes various foibles of the black American middle class. Nevertheless, as she indicated in an unpublished section of her essay "The New Paternalists," she carefully controlled her attack to ensure that it "is not in terms that deny his *right* to exist but is merely critical of the *absurdities* of his values." These values are largely those of the money-obsessed and business-oriented sectors of the middle class of any race: a delight in luxury and status, slavish attachment to the latest fashion, contempt for the aims and abilities of the lower class, conformity to a rigid code of social behavior, and pragmatic indifference to knowledge for its own sake:

"You read books—to learn facts—to get grades—to pass the course—to get a degree. . . . it has nothing to do with thoughts." Murchison does, however, make one additional mistake that Hansberry viewed as a special failing of large sections of the black middle class, as it was among the middle class of other ethnic groups. He dissociates himself from the culture of his own race, both African and African American. As Hansberry noted in "The Negro Writer and His Roots," "A minute and well-groomed black bourgeoisie [middle class] is cautious of the implications of a true love of the folk heritage. Sophistication allows the listening of spirituals if performed by concert artists, but in church—[J.S.] Bach chorales and [George Frideric] Handel, please!"

Murchison is the one true assimilationist in the play; the piece of cultural knowledge that he prizes most is that "in New York standard" theater "curtain time is eight forty." Hansberry saw a grain of hope even in a George Murchison, however. The Broadway script of *A Raisin in the Sun* included a scene (cut at the last minute and restored in the twenty-fifth anniversary and "American Playhouse" editions) in which Murchison, after initially disapproving of Beneatha's new, unfashionable Afro hairstyle, suddenly finds himself liking it. The stage directions concerning his expression of approval "thoughtful, with emphasis, since this is a reversal" underline his amazement—and his capacity for change.

Murchison, Asagai, and the Black Middle Class

Significantly, Hansberry conceived of Asagai, for all his differences in attitude from Murchison, as a member of his middle class. In an unpublished letter dated February 3, 1959, to a professor of American studies who had apparently taken literally Asagai's whimsical speech to Beneatha about the "African Prince" come to sweep the "maiden" back to the country of her ancestors, Hansberry commented:

A matter of information: the character Joseph Asagai, the African student, has mystically achieved "princehood" in your mind. That rather amused me because his specific family background is not described in the play. . . . but I have always envisioned him more closely to a product of the rising colonial bourgeoisie of Nigeria; which, in my mind, would account for his progressive viewpoint more logically. . . . The young man to me represents intellect; warm and free and confident. These have always seemed to me the primary characteristics of certain colonials I have known from India and West Africa. They generally have the magnificence of actively insurgent peoples along with the sophisticated ease of those who are preoccupied with the eventual possession of the future. Despair cannot afflict this man in these years; he has ascertained the nature of political despotism and seen in it not the occasion for cynicism—but an ever growing sense of how the new will never cease to replace the old. He thinks man and history are marvelous on account of this view. Finally, it is my own view.

Hansberry clearly understood that class attitudes are shaped by time, culture, and circumstance so that, in 1959, the black, middle-class Nigerian more nearly resembled in some important respects the more insurgent outlook of the black working class than his supposed African-American middle-class counterpart. Thus, in an early draft, when Beneatha argues that Asagai's "faith [in man, in revolution, in liberation, in the possibility of changing the world] is worse than Mama's. And just as blind," he responds, "I suppose it is very similar." One of Hansberry's wishes (which her own example supported to the limited extent that any individual's can) was that the Murchisons of the future would, through the pressures of circumstance and the aspirations and actions of a multitude of Younger families, become closer in spirit to the Asagais of the late fifties and early sixties. Actually, many Murchisons did get involved in the civil rights struggle in the sixties, and contemporary Murchisons are generally more respectful of their African heritage (now that it is fashionable), although, torn between the need for continuing struggle and strong pressures to conform, they remain uneasily and waveringly wedded to the system.

Racism and Sexism

As her encounters with Walter, Murchison, and Asagai indicate, Beneatha has had to contend with innumerable insults and attempted limitations from sexism as well as from racism. Her crisis at the end of the play comes from the realization that, with the loss of the money that she had counted on to complete her education, her life-long struggle may prove to have been futile, that the combined restrictions on women, blacks, and the poor may finally enclose her. This aspect of her despair is strongly implied in the play as it stands, but was neatly and ironically spelled out in an early draft in which Beneatha tells Asagai:

> You endure knowing that in fifteen years of education every single time you have spoken of medicine, someone in an office somewhere has immediately advised you, with a cultured voice and a charming smile, to take up typing—or Home Economics.
>
> You endure.... And you begin to think that you are very strong. But the comedy comes—when you think you have overcome these things—
>
> It is only then that you begin to wonder about life. What kind of sense it will ever make when it is possible for your brother to hand away your future to a man—who will, undoubtedly, spend it on women who long ago gave up the hope of overcoming anything at all.

Beneatha and Walter

In spite of these special problems she has faced as a woman and other differences stemming from her education and idealism, Beneatha is essentially very similar to Walter. This similarity is accentuated in the stage directions which introduce her, noting that she is "as slim and intense as her brother." It is further emphasized by the way he shares her fantasy about being African. (In an early draft, Lena, responding to an attack by Beneatha on colonialism, observes, "Lord, now you sound just like your brother when he was about your age. For a while there he was all interested in these people who get out on the streets on them ladders and talk about Africa all the time.") Moreover, she and her brother are both driven by egotism to get as much of the insurance money as possible for their personal goals; Beneatha is just as ready to cut her brother out of any share in the money as he is to cut her out. They also respond to the loss of the money in roughly equivalent ways; the stage directions, after stressing the aloneness and disappointment of each, continue, "We see on a line from her brother's bedroom the sameness of their attitudes." Like Walter, she rises out of her despair to make an active commitment to the white-surrounded house, thereby gaining a corresponding sense of solidarity with her family. Both of them, however, retain their personal goals for the future, she of becoming a doctor, he of going into some business; they have simply established a set of priorities, placing the family and the struggle for the house first.

All of these resemblances suggest—intentionally—that men and women differ far less than traditional views would have us believe, that many of the "differences" are artificially induced by their cultures rather than inherent. Of course, cultural distinctions can have serious consequences, leading to privilege for one group and oppression for another, but the underlying similarities in human nature remove all justification for such differing treatment. Beneatha and Walter rightly come to see that their real opponents are not each other but the entire system of privilege and exclusion based on many false distinctions.

Beneatha's Selfishness

Unfortunately, Hansberry's vigorous, sharp, and usually in-
triguing characterization of Beneatha is slightly marred by her
one serious artistic misstep in *A Raisin in the Sun*. This occurs
when Beneatha tells Lena and Ruth about the guitar lessons
she has just started and they remind her about "the horseback-
riding club for which she bought that fifty-five dollar riding
habit that's been hanging in the closet ever since!" On the
whole, this scene portrays Beneatha's striving for self-
expression with warm humor and a touch of self-mockery
that almost always please audiences. The problem is that only
a short time earlier Walter had angrily demanded that Beneatha show more gratitude for the financial sacrifices he and
Ruth have made for her, and Ruth had denied her son the 50
cents he requested for school. It is inconceivable that a woman
who could refuse such a small sum to a dearly beloved son
would so casually accept the squandering of a much larger
contribution to a mere sister-in-law, and even if, by some
miracle, she were able to accept it out of an all-embracing
feminist sisterhood (which doesn't fit Ruth's overall character),
she could not do so with such ease. Worse still, lightly tossing
away all this money in the face of the family's dire need makes
Beneatha seem monstrously selfish rather than mildly selfish
as Hansberry had intended. Granted, Hansberry's main concern in the scene was the general relationship between the two
older women and Beneatha, particularly their fond amuse-
ment at the younger woman's forms of self-expression, which
are so different from anything they have ever done, and their
vicarious delight at her ability to break free from restrictions,
including that of having to weigh the cost of everything. However, on this rare occasion, by concentrating exclusively on the
moment and neglecting to see its relation to previous parts of
the play, Hansberry, to a small but disconcerting extent, damages the whole. Ironically, the scene also proved a small stum-
bling block for Robert Nemiroff and Charlotte Zaltzberg in a

different way in their book for the musical *Raisin*. While they recognized the problem in having Beneatha throw away money and solved it by having her take up such uncostly activities as a world government group and weaving as her forms of expression, they also chose an antivivisection [opposition to medical research on animals] league as one of the forms, a choice contradicted—if we assume she was serious at all in her remark—by her earlier flippant comment to Walter that in biology class she "dissected something—. . . looked just like *you*."

A *Raisin in the Sun* Is a Protest Against Homophobia

Karen Ocamb

Karen Ocamb is the news editor for Frontiers in LA *magazine, a publication for the lesbian, gay, bisexual, and transgender community in Los Angeles. She has contributed to numerous media outlets, including the* Los Angeles Times, TV Guide Online, *the* Advocate, *and* OutQ News *on Sirius Satellite Radio.*

In the following selection, Ocamb writes of her discussion with the coproducer of the February 2008 television production of A Raisin in the Sun, *starring rapper and entrepreneur Sean "P. Diddy" Combs. When Craig Zadan and his coproducer, Neil Meron, saw the revival of the play on Broadway, they realized that* Raisin *had been brought alive for a new generation of theatergoers and decided to produce it as a television movie. Ocamb writes that Zadan understands the play's central theme of racism to be a vehicle for another type of prejudice—homophobia. According to Zadan, as a closeted lesbian, Lorraine Hansberry understood well the various forms of discrimination minority groups in America suffer from. In the film, Beneatha, who represents Hansberry herself, passionately defends her right to live the way she wants to. Ocamb explains that Zadan sees a gay subtext here and argues that Hansberry was far ahead of her time in crying out against homophobia as well as against racism.*

Let's be honest: most people will probably tune into ABC's drama *A Raisin in the Sun* tonight [February 5, 2008,] to see if Sean "P-Diddy" Combs can act. He can. In fact, the entire cast is achingly brilliant.

And with the 40th anniversaries of the assassinations of Rev. Martin Luther King Jr. and Sen. Robert F. Kennedy

Karen Ocamb, "*A Raisin in the Sun* Producer Craig Zadan on the Movie's Gay Subtext," *The Huffington Post*, February 5, 2008. Reproduced by permission of the author.

coming up—and the new "I have a dream" candidate Barack Obama trying to turn a political campaign into a movement for social change, many might think that the dream deferred—the "raisin" of the title from black gay poet Langston Hughes' poem "Harlem" ("What happens to a dream deferred?/Does it dry up/like a raisin in the sun?")—is outdated.

Racism, Sexism, and Homophobia

It's not. Racism is still rampant, the film's gay co-producer Craig Zadan points out. So is homophobia and the closet—one of the subtexts of the original play written by African American lesbian Lorraine Hansberry.

Lorraine Hansbery "is one of the most famous lesbian playwrights who nobody knew was a lesbian," Zadan told me by phone as he drove to a press conference with Combs at the Hollywood Foreign Press Association.

Of course, Hansberry is now famous among African American LGBT [lesbian, gay, bisexual, and transgender] people. But in her time—especially in 1959 when *Raisin in the Sun* became the first play written by a black woman to be produced on Broadway—Hansberry qualified as the kind of woman [English] artist Virginia Woolf talked about in her famous 1928 Cambridge lecture, "Shakespeare's sister."

All these elements—racism, sexism, and homophobia—occurred to Zadan and his producing partner Neil Meron (also openly gay) at Storyline Entertainment when they saw the revival of *A Raisin in the Sun* on Broadway with the same cast that's in the ABC movie. The producing partners have a long history of consciously using diversity in theme and casting.

Producing *Raisin in the Sun*

Zadan explained the process by which they brought the play to television and Hansberry's gay subtext.

Craig Zadan and co-producer Neil Meron attempted to emphasize Hansberry's homosexual subtext in their 2008 television production of A Raisin in the Sun. *Pictured are co-stars Sanaa Lathan, Phylicia Rashad, Audra McDonald, Justin Martin, and Sean 'P. Diddy' Combs. Sanaa Lathan, plays Beneatha, whom Zadan sees as a stand-in for Hansberry herself, who is exploring lesbianism from a political point of view.* ABC-TV/The Kobal Collection/Alston, Kuaku.

Neil and I have been drawn to movies that fall into three distinct groups: One is musicals, which we took upon ourselves to try to bring back when nobody was doing musicals; the second is bio-pics. When no one was doing bio-pics, we, on TV, we did Judy Garland, the Beach Boys, the Reagans—a whole lot of biographical things; and the third—social and political films like *Serving in Silence, What Makes a Family,* and *Wedding Wars,* which are gay and lesbian stories. We're always developing more, looking for more social/political stories.

We went to see the revival [of *Raisin* on Broadway] when it opened a couple of years ago and we were just blown away by it. We realized that Sean Combs made it feel contemporary. The audience was comprised of the youngest people we've ever seen at a play. The place was packed with Caucasians and African Americans—but kids and families. We'd never seen an audience like that ever on Broadway for a straight dramatic play. And they went nuts. They went to see it—maybe—because of Diddy—but they came away having had that experience of this piece with that cast. And we were determined at that point that we wanted to turn it into a movie.

Luckily our deal is at Sony and luckily Sony [Columbia Pictures] made the original *Raisin in the Sun* with [American actor Sidney] Poitier. So we lucked out. We went to them and everybody embraced it. And then we went to Steve McPherson [president of ABC Entertainment] and we didn't even get the words out of our mouth and he jumped up and said, 'Go make it now.' He immediately understood how important the story was and with that cast. He said, 'You get that cast—go make the picture.'

Unfortunately it took us two years because those actors—Audra McDonald, Phylicia Rashad, Sanaa Lathan, Sean Combs—are so busy with plays and movies and concert tours. It took us two years to coordinate schedules.

Finally, last year [in 2007] they all said to us, 'OK, we have between Thanksgiving and Christmas Eve—so we'll give you that,' We were freaking out because we were still shooting *Hairspray*, we were about to start shooting *The Bucket List*—so we said, 'You know what—it's really hard to pull this off right now. But we're not even going to think about it. We're just going to pull it off.'

So we immediately set up production—in many cases working seven days a week—because we had to finish in that tiny, tiny window.

We made it happen in Toronto because we were finishing *Hairspray* in Toronto and we couldn't leave the city.

We finished the movie and then Neil and I edited it very quickly. But ABC said, 'You know what—this is too important. We can't throw this on the air. Work with us—be patient and let's give it a coveted time slot.'

And everybody was like, 'We want to put it on now.' They said, 'No—trust us.' We said, 'OK.' They basically said, 'We think we should hold it until next year and put it on the night after the Oscars so we can promote it during the Academy Awards,' which is of course the largest audience watching ABC all year. So we used last night [Oscar night] as a platform and we're on tonight.

A Story About Racism

But Neil and I—when we saw it we said, 'This is very, very important.' The truth of the matter is—when we look at things—every movie we do—no matter what the subject matter is—we go to the universal theme of family. We always go to that because if the movie is about family, then any audience can relate to it. We feel that this one—more than just about any of them—is about what happens to a family falling apart and disintegrating and pulling itself back together again.

We felt its was a very important African American story, a very important story about racism. Some people said, 'Oh—

this is 1969.' And 'Yes—but what about [*Seinfeld* actor] Michael Richard [profusely using the "n-word" during a stand-up routine at the Laugh Factory in Los Angeles] and [radio shock jock] Don Imus [who got briefly kicked off the air for calling the Rutgers Women's basketball team "nappy-headed hos"] and what about Jena—that town where they hung nooses [a tactic used to intimidate African Americans]? So everything going on around us was all about blatant racism.

And then on top of all that—out of the blue—came Barack Obama, which we didn't anticipate. So we felt there was this amazing story that needed to be told today because racism is rampant in America and needs to be dealt with—and dealt with not standing on a soapbox preaching but by moving people to tears and breaking their hearts—that's how you reach people.

The Gay Subtext

But that jumps off to another point: whenever you deal with an issue of minorities, you also deal with gays and lesbians—and especially here with a play by an African American lesbian playwright—it became very, very important to us to tell this story.

We think there are some subliminal things going on that [you'll see] if you watch the movie. You get into these people's lives and you are as moved as we were by their story and by the actors. We think people will get it since it deals with minorities, it deals with race, it deals with prejudice, it deals with everything in the world today.

What I found particularly interesting was that beyond racism are other prejudices. You have everybody trying to hush up about the fact that [Hansberry] was a lesbian playwright. I think part of it comes from the fact that she had a heterosexual marriage. I'm sure it was a loving relationship and I'm sure they cared about each other a great deal. But the point is—when that marriage came to an end, we found out where her heart was.

[Hansberry] wrote a lot of lesbian political stories in different publications and at that time signed it "LH." So she was willing to write constantly about the gay and lesbian cause but at the same time, she was never willing to sign her real name to it. Talk about the closet—I think that's amazing.

It is very, very important that people understand that you can tell different kinds of stories and they do relate to gay and lesbian issues—especially when you know the people behind them.

Lorraine Hansberry was clearly writing from the gay experience. The character that Sanaa Lathan plays [Beneatha] is the Lorraine Hansberry character. She represents Lorraine. If you look at the ideas and you look at what she had to say and how outspoken she is and how she's breaking traditions and breaking rules and being rebellious and experimenting—you can look at that very clearly as her exploring her lesbianism, from a political point of view. Even though she's talking about other things, beneath the surface you can see what she's really talking about. So I think if you watch the movie and you know that Sanaa Lathan is playing Lorraine Hansberry's character, expressing Lorraine's point of view—you then start to see the ramifications of the gay and lesbian experience screaming to come out.

She was so prescient that she was telling us about the Women's Liberation Movement, the gay and lesbian movement and the civil rights movement—before these movements happened. She was a young girl. How could somebody 27 years old have the insight to understand—it's one thing if she wrote a trilogy or if she wrote 10 plays—but in one play to express all of those issues and values? It's astonishing.

And we're so used to writing where every so often there is a great line. Not in this—almost every line counts. And if you understand the subtext of what she's really saying, you realize how political and powerful her message is. So any gay or lesbian viewer would get so much out of it and understand how deeply and how powerful and how emotional and how ahead of her time she was; it took a lesbian to tell the world that the world was changing.

Mama Lena Is an Acceptable Tyrant

Trudier Harris

Trudier Harris is the J. Carlyle Sitterson Professor Emerita at the University of North Carolina at Chapel Hill, where she taught courses in African American literature and folklore. Her books include From Mammies to Militants: Domestics in Black American Literature, Exorcising Blackness: Historical and Literary Lynching and Burning Rituals, *and* South of Tradition: Essays on African American Literature.

By virtue of her size and her title of "Mama Lena," Lena Younger is an imposing figure in the household, Harris explains in the following selection. She controls her family in a manner that combines emotional and physical intimidation. Such methods could have offended audiences and caused critical concern, but this response was not widespread. Audiences that were more concerned with inter-racial politics than intra-racial politics were content to overlook Mama's bullying ways, Harris asserts, viewing her brand of domestic violence as acceptable in a culture that was well acclimated to the concept of the domineering black matriarch.

With Davis' comments as a point of departure and, in a less excited time, with clearer critical insight, it can be argued that Mama Lena Younger is as much a problem in the lives of her family as whites are, and her influence is more immediate and perhaps operates at a more insidious level. The source of that problem is her strength, which begins with her name and her physical size and is very quickly bolstered by her Christianity. Hansberry herself gave Mama Lena the designation of matriarch, asserting that Mama Lena is "The Black matriarch incarnate: The bulwark of the Negro family since slavery; the embodiment of the Negro will to transcendence. It is she who, in the mind of the Black poet, scrubs the floors of a nation in order to create Black diplomats and university professors. It is she who, while seeming to cling to traditional restraints, drives the young on into the fire hoses and one day simply refuses to move to the back of the bus in Montgomery."[9] Hansberry is perhaps more altruistic in the description of the matriarch than, as I will illustrate, her own characterization of Mama Lena warrants, for Mama Lena's good intentions are frequently overshadowed by the strong-armed methods she uses to achieve her objectives. Notably, however, Hansberry did admit the tendency to tyranny inherent in such figures, and she finds this possibility acceptable when measured against the ultimate good intentions of such women historically: "Not that there aren't negative things about it [the strong mother], and not that tyranny sometimes doesn't emerge as part of it. But basically it's a *great* thing. These women have the backbone of our people in a very necessary way."[10] Doris Abramson supports Hansberry's assessment by naming Mama Lena, as did original reviewer Tom F. Driver, "a tyrannical but good-natured matriarch."[11] J. Charles Washington, writing in the 1980s, refers to Mama Lena's "overpowering personality . . . particularly her moral rectitude and selfless nature."[12] Hansberry biographer Margaret B. Wilkerson recognizes Mama Lena's mold in the stereotypical, but suggests that Mama Lena breaks out of the mold.

> Mama, who initially fits the popular stereotype of the Black Mammy, *seems* to be the domineering head of household. She rules everyone's life. . . . Mammy gives way to the caring, understanding mother, historic cornerstone of the black family. . . . While Mama may *seem* to be merely conservative, clinging to an older generation, it is she who, in fact, is

the mother of revolutionaries; it is she who makes possible the change and movement of the new generation [emphasis mine].[13]

In these assessments, tyranny is altruistic. It begins, I argue, with a name. In the historical tradition from which her character is drawn, a woman like Mrs. Lena Younger would seldom be referred to as "Mrs. Younger." Instead, nonrelatives would usually call her "Miss Lena," and family members would adopt appropriate respectful titles. The honorary and respectful "Mama" designates a role and family position as well as a size (even the way those "m"s spread out in "M-a-m-a" seems to support this size argument). "Big Mamas," "Ma-maws," and "Nanas" populate the African American literary and historical landscapes and generally refer to black women who are usually third—but sometimes fourth and fifth—generation heads of households. These women, mostly widowed but sometimes married to mousy men who seldom earn the comparable appellation of "Big Papa," mind the business of *all* their family members.[14] From the perspective of their grandchildren, the title "Mama" makes clear that the authority of these women applies to but also by-passes their own offspring and has a direct impact upon this third generation. No one who is in the second generation of such a triad can expect to assert about a grandchild, "This is my child. I will tell him what to do," and believe that "Mama" is going to take it seriously. "Mama" highlights the biological connection across generations, thus demonstrating that authority follows biology and will not be interrupted by skipping a generation. The designation enables grandmothers like Mama Lena to engage directly with the third generation and dominate them usually as much and sometimes more than the second generation. It is important to note that the Youngers are sharecropper migrants from Mississippi. They would thus have been heir to southern factors that give rise to the creation of black family generations.[15]

It is no coincidence that the physically large Claudia Mc-Neil was selected to play the role of Mama Lena Younger on the stage as well as in the 1961 Columbia Pictures film version of the play, for the mimetic quality extended from subject matter and characterization to cast selection.[16] Hansberry's description of Mama Lena probably influenced the selection of McNeil as well:

> *MAMA* enters. She is a woman in her early sixties, full-bodied and *strong*. She is one of those women of a certain grace and beauty who wear it so unobtrusively that it takes a while to notice. Her dark-brown face is surrounded by the total whiteness of her hair, and being a woman who has adjusted to many things in life and overcome many more, her face is full of *strength*[17] .

Throughout the play, Mama Lena's size and physical strength are focal points for action. On stage, Mama Lena towered over the women cast as Ruth and Beneatha; photographs from those productions make the contrasts strikingly obvious. In reading the play, her sheer force of will is apparent in contrast to everyone around her as it looms larger and carries more force. Body size and strength of character simultaneously operate to locate Mama Lena in the stereotype of the domineering strong black woman character as well as to lift her slightly out of it because she is literally the prototype for what later would be judged to be stereotypical.

This size factor is especially important in the scene that sets Mama Lena's biological tyranny in bas relief, that is, in the scene in which she slaps Beneatha for denying the existence of God. When Beneatha ends a tirade with 'There simply is no blasted God—there is only man and it is he who makes miracles!," "(MAMA *absorbs this speech, studies her daughter and rises slowly and crosses to* BENEATHA *and slaps her powerfully across the face. After, there is only silence and the daughter drops her eyes from her mother's face, and MAMA is very tall before her*)." (39) Mama Lena combines physical size with moral strength when she forces Beneatha to repeat after her: "Now—you say after me, in my mother's house there is still God." (39) The reluctant Beneatha repeats the phrase in spite of her unwillingness to do so. And although Mama is *"too disturbed for triumphant posture"* as she leaves the scene, she has nonetheless made her point about where power resides in the family and who shapes reality. But she is not too disturbed to say as she departs: "There are some ideas we ain't going to have in this house. Not long as I am at the head of this family," and Beneatha meekly replies, "Yes, ma'am". (39) Mama Lena's way of looking at the universe is reinstated, verbally and physically if not substantively, and, in this setting, the physical forcing of verbal acquiescence seems to carry the day. As J. Charles Washington points out, Mama Lena's "actions rarely receive censure even though they are far less than ideal."[18] As African American scholar SallyAnn Ferguson asserts, the violence Mama Lena exhibits is an acceptable dimension of the woman in this tradition who is in charge of her household.[19] Ruth adds her brick to the wall of the status quo by asserting to Mama Lena after Beneatha's departure: "You just got strong-willed children and it takes a strong woman like you to keep 'em in hand" (40) a comment that encompasses the physical and the moral.

Mama's logic in reaction to Beneatha's blasphemy is centered upon the belief that no child borne of her body could have strayed so far from the moral values of its mother, a concept tied to the biblical notion that like trees bear like fruit ("By their fruits ye shall know them"). Beneatha therefore cannot remain unrecognizable because she has come from a recognizable source, thus Mama Lena presumably slaps her back into that familiar recognition. It is the "Mama" position that has given Mama Lena the "right" to slap Beneatha, thereby making name, size, biology, and morality equal parts of the authority she wields.[20] Beneatha might assert after Mama Lena leaves the scene, "I see also that everybody thinks it's all right for Mama to be a tyrant. But all the tyranny in the world will never put a God in the heavens!" (40) but *in Mama Lena's presence*, Beneatha does as she is told.[21] Neither she nor Walter has the will to stand toe-to-toe, so to speak, with Mama, state a case, and win an argument. Mama's physical and moral power *as mother* are not to be challenged. She usually gets little resistance when she insists upon imposing her view of reality upon her family.

Mama Lena is like a hurricane that carves its path through any obstacles it encounters. That force, guided by the same attributes that determine her behavior with Beneatha, enables her to direct the lives of Travis, Ruth, and Walter Lee. . . .

Mama Lena is in her 60s, and Hansberry writes that she is still a beautiful woman. In the current action of the play, however, she has no gentleman caller(s) and seems thoroughly devoted to the memory of Big Walter.[32] It is worthwhile to examine the legend of that relationship, for Mama Lena uses it in several instances to coerce her family to certain attitudes and actions. Though no mention of church going occurs in the current action of the play, Mama Lena comments, when she is confronted with Beneatha's blasphemy, that she and Big Walter took the children to Sunday School every Sunday; that memory is intended as a weapon to inspire Beneatha to toe the proper religious line. Mama Lena also uses Big Walter's example to inspire Walter Lee to accept his responsibility to Ruth and their unborn child, and memory of Big Walter's hard work provides the emotional depth of the betrayal when Walter Lee gives the money away. Yet what of the intimate relationship between Mama Lena and Big Walter? Has he been only a provider and concerned father? What of the privacy of their relationship? Certainly they had sex, but was there any romance there? Part of her heightened reaction to Ruth's contemplation of abortion is memory of the death of little Claude and how Big Walter responded to that tragedy. But that is precisely the area of concern in relation to her strength, for Mama

Lena charts Big Walter's reaction to the death more so than her own, as if her strength has enabled her to endure the loss better than her husband—in spite of the child having issued from her very body.

More important, by making Big Walter larger than life, she diminishes his faults, and it is in those faults that we gauge what she has given up—or been forced to endure—in their relationship. She says: "Crazy 'bout his children! God knows there was plenty wrong with Walter Younger—hardheaded, mean, kind of wild with women—plenty wrong with him. But he sure loved his children. Always wanted them to have something—be something." (33) Mama Lena's intimate relationship with her husband is buried in the set aside phrase where she names his faults. What did his "hardheadedness" mean for her as his wife? How did his "meanness" affect her and indeed their children? And is "kind of wild with women" another one of those toning down expressions to which Mama Lena resorts to alter reality? Consider a couple of examples. When Walter Lee is suffering through the constant deferral of his dreams, he implores her, "I want so many things that they are driving me kind of crazy . . . Mama—look at me," with the clear intent of her seeing his pain. Rather than comply, she turns his anguish and his potential serious meaning in a superficial direction: "I'm looking at you. You a good-looking boy. You got a job, a nice wife, a fine boy and—." (60) Later, when the money is gone, she exaggerates the family's ability to make do in the space in which they currently live: "Been thinking 'bout some of the things we could do to fix this place up some. I seen a second-hand bureau over on Maxwell Street just the other day that could fit right there. . . . Would need some new handles on it and then a little varnish and then it look like something brand-new." (129) As Audre Lorde says her mother taught her, when you cannot change reality, change your attitude toward reality. Mama Lena can change reality on occasions, but she definitely changes her attitude toward it.

These exaggerations and potential for changing reality thus raise questions about her relationship with Big Walter. How many women was he wild about? How frequently? And what kind of impact did infidelity have upon this strong black woman, in spite of her ability to contain it under her husband's ostensible love for his children. Whatever happened in the relationship with Big Walter, its relegation to memory now makes it pristine, and it makes Mama Lena's fidelity loom even larger.

In other words, by not showing any interest in men, Mama Lena is a *respectable* woman, so respectable that she does not even think of what it would mean to have a male companion/lover. And the setting of the play complicates that consideration. Where on earth would she and a man be intimate? While Hansberry allows for the modicum of privacy that Walter Lee and Ruth are able to have by allowing them a room to themselves, Mama Lena must share her room and bed with Beneatha, thus Hansberry has written out of the text any possibility for Mama Lena to have the privacy necessary to romantic relationships. By contrast, think again of Eva Peace in Morrison's *Sula*. Eva might be less than respectable by church ladies' estimations, but she refuses to deny her sensuality or her need for male companionship; even with one leg, she has several gentlemen callers. For Mama Lena, the lack of consideration of the potential intimate/romantic part of her humanity merely places her more solidly into the self-sacrificial role of strong black women characters. Give up men. Give up sex. Give up privacy. Give up any thoughts of the flesh not immediately related to eating in preparation for work or feeling tired in response to work. Devote oneself exclusively to family. In exchange, earn the right to manage them with little course-changing objection.

Within as well as beyond her family, however, Mama Lena is a loner. That, too, is a serious consequence for the strong black woman character. As mostly undisputed head of her household, Mama Lena obviously has no peer. The hierarchy of power established within the family illustrates clearly that she has no one on earth to whom she can turn—even if she wanted to—for consultation about the decisions she makes. She might *look* "pleadingly" at her children and daughter-in-law on a couple of occasions to get them to *accept* her decisions, but she does not consult them in the decision-making process. Her position and power leave her without a shoulder to cry on, without a designated sympathetic soul mate. On the first brief occasion when she seems to falter (when she admits that she has been wrong and helped to hurt Walter Lee as much as the larger society has hurt him), she even argues with him in taking blame. "I been wrong," she says, to which Walter Lee, probably sarcastically, responds: "Naw, you ain't never been wrong about nothing, Mama." Still going it alone, she retorts: "Listen to me, now. I say I been wrong, son." (86) On the second brief occasion when she appears to falter—after Walter Lee has lost the money—she still has no worldly soul confessor to whom she can take her burden. Instead, she adopts another directive posture and orders the family to begin unpacking the things they have packed in preparation for the move. Even when she is apparently *"lost, vague, trying to catch hold, to make some sense of her former command of the world,"* (118) she does not share that lostness with anyone; she continues to make decisions in spite of her seemingly diminished state. True to one of the primary tenets of the strong black woman character, she keeps on keeping on, more alone than not.

Another consequence of Mama Lena's strength that has a direct impact upon her physical well being is her size itself. Her large body is an indication of diet, which suggests that it is not one most conducive to good health. While Mama Lena is still strong and still able to work as a domestic, there are blatant signals in the text that her working days are limited. It could be argued that size is as much a factor as age in this anticipated conclusion to her working years. The acquisition of that size fits again into diet and the health issues surrounding the insistence in black communities that size is a reflection of strength and health. Mama Lena is as much concerned about food and the size of those around her as are the women in those historical communities. Remember her wanting Travis' oats loaded down with "lots of butter" (29) as well as her comment that Beneatha might catch a cold because she is "so thin," (28) and she is eager to prepare "some homecooked meals" (32) for Asagai.

Finally, the psychological pain that Mama Lena inflicts upon others is also hers to bear. That is apparent in her reaction to Beneatha's disbelief, in Walter Lee's refusal to be the man Mama Lena envisioned concerning the proposed abortion, and in her disappointment when Walter Lee gives away the insurance money. Those scenes pale, however, in comparison to those in which she is strong and dominating. By sheer volume of representation, the emphasis is on the side of seeming psychological health, so that the minor rips in that tightly worn garment are quickly repaired. The tight reins that Mama Lena holds on her family only *almost* unravel in her hands. I emphasize almost here because the strong black woman character seems always to recover, and that is no less the case with Mama Lena.

She is *the* classic example of the problematic nature of the black female character's strength. Mama Lena was so well-received in 1959 precisely because blacks were more concerned about *inter*racial issues than *intra*racial issues. If a strong black woman character like Mama Lena could make the case for acceptability of all black people, then why quibble, as one of the reviewers asserted, over her excesses of characterization? The facts that she was on stage, recognizable, and representative were sufficient unto themselves.

Since Walter, Ruth, Beneatha, and Travis all seem to respect Mama Lena, another question arises. If her way of raising them is so troubling to close readers, and if she has such an insidious impact upon them, why is their response to her not more negative? I would argue that, in the mold of expectation and community imperative that governs Mama Lena's behavior, the same governs her children. They cannot ultimately reject the impact of her parenting because they are also drawn to reflect a particular time and place: the circle of acceptability that informs their historical counterparts also informs Hansberry's creation of them. The culture has taught them to respect Mama Lena, in spite of her tyranny, just as it has taught her to throw her weight around. But in terms of her impact upon them, imagine the other characters beyond the time frame of the play. Walter is probably still going to be dependent upon the women. Beneatha will probably become a doctor, perhaps more in spite of than because of Mama Lena. And Ruth is still going to be mousy. Travis is a question mark, but he has seen enough of how his family operates to know that women are dominant, men have little power, and his father has had to acquiesce to Mama Lena's wishes in order to win her approval.

The play-going audiences' acceptance of Mama Lena's excesses depended in large part on what I call a communal moral imperative. As I mentioned earlier, the general consensus was that the majority of "Negroes" at the time were religious, did not believe in abortion, were aware of if not acquiescent in various forms of domestic violence (especially in terms of parents disciplining children), and accepted all the foregoing as the norm. Indeed, this was a period in African American history that one could conceivably refer to "the black community," for—primarily due to racial positioning—views were more consistent than divergent. Consequently, black people joined with whites in finding the physically and religiously comforting image of Mama Lena acceptable in spite of her violence and invasions of privacy. As Ossie Davis pointed out, the mere fact that this recognizable black woman character made it to the stage satisfied just about everybody. Therefore, the average black person viewing the play, or for whom the play was written, probably did not pause very long—if at all—to meditate on the fact that Hansberry had joined with many white writers in portraying African American women, with slight modifications, in a particular stereotypical way. Her collaboration was just as effective as those earlier ones in which black actresses played the stereotyped roles assigned to them. Through Hansberry's tremendously effective portrayal, then, blacks and whites fell in love with Mama Lena, who, despite her tyranny, served as a source of comfort to both groups.

Notes

9. Quoted in Steven R. Carter, *Hansberry's Drama: Commitment amid Complexity* (Urbana and Chicago: University of Illinois Press, 1991), pp. 52–53.

10. Quoted in Carter, *Hansberry's Drama*, p. 53.

11. Doris E. Abramson, *Negro Playwrights in the American Theater 1925–1959* (New York and London: Columbia University Press, 1969), p. 254. Less generous in his assessment of characters and play is Harold Cruse, who dubbed *Raisin* a "glorified soap opera" in which Hansberry forcibly ascribes middle-class values to a lower-working-class family to make them acceptable as integrationists. See *The Crisis of the Negro Intellectual* (New York: Morrow, 1967), pp. 267–284.

12. 'A Raisin in the Sun' Revisited," *Black American Literature Forum* 22:1 (Spring 1988): 110–111.

13. "The Sighted Eyes and Feeling Heart of Lorraine Hansberry," *Black American Literature Forum* 17:1 (Spring 1983): 10.

14. Mama Lena's deceased husband is occasionally referred to as "Big Walter," a distinction designed to separate him

from "little" Walter Lee and not necessarily one that designates authority in relation to his wife or other family members.

15. "The Mama" designation is also visible in Mama Lena insinuating herself into a motherly role to Asagai. She immediately assumes that, with him being so far away from home, he needs a nurturing surrogate mother's love; "I bet you don't half look after yourself, being away from your mama either. I spec you better come 'round here from time to time and get yourself some decent homecooked meals . . ." (52). Historical mamas are noted for playing this role, but even Mama Lena lays it on thick for a first encounter with Asagai.

16. Other members of the cast appearing on stage and in the film included Sidney Poitier (Walter Lee), Diana Sands (Beneatha), Ruby Dee (Ruth), Glynn Turman (Travis), Louis Gossett (George Murchison), and Ivan Dixon (Asagai). Although Hansberry wrote two screenplays and new and substantially different scenes for the film, none of the new material was used. Carter points out that the film "was basically a shortened version of the play." Still, "the final product was good enough to earn a nomination for Best Screenplay of the Year from the Screenwriters Guild and a Special award at the Cannes Film Festival, both in 1961" ("Hansberry," p. 128). A second film version of the play, produced for television in 1989, featured Esther Rolle as Mama Lena Younger and Danny Glover as Walter Lee Younger; other cast members included Kim Yancy (Beneatha), Starletta DuPois (Ruth), and Kimble Joyner (Travis). The play was also transformed into a musical, *Raisin*, that appeared on Broadway in 1973 and has had many reprisals since then.

17. Lorraine Hansberry, *A Raisin in the Sun* (New York: Signet, 1966), p. 27, my emphasis. Notice that, although Hansberry emphasizes Mama Lena's beauty as much as she

does her strength (in the sentences quoted and those immediately following), Mama Lena's beauty is never a factor in the play, while her physical and moral strength undergird most of the action.

18. "*A Raisin in the Sun* Revisited," 111.

19. Ferguson argues that Mama Lena's violence should "lead to an examination of African American views on corporal punishment—where such practice is not viewed as abusive and tyrannical but corrective and loving. It's in the Christian tradition of violence as redemption. (Jesus hangs to save mankind.) Ruth uses the threat of a beating to keep Travis in line, too." Personal communication to the author, January 1997. From a different perspective than my own, therefore, Ferguson's comment connects nicely to the Christian basis for the actions of strong black women characters.

20. While it could be argued that the parent/child dynamic is reflective of 1950s historical black reality, in which children were expected to be "seen and not heard," that argument is flawed by the fact that, though she may treat them otherwise, both of Mama Lena's "children" are biologically—if not emotionally or economically—adults.

21. As many scholars have noted, Beneatha's very name places her in a lesser position, "beneath her," to Mama Lena.

32. A flaw in the play is the uncertainty about how much time has elapsed since Big Walter's death. The family seems ensconced and comfortable in its current relational and sleeping arrangements. Where, for example, did Beneatha sleep before Big Walter died, since she is now in his place in bed with Mama Lena? Did Travis sleep in the room with his parents before Big Walter's death and Beneatha on the couch? How long did it take for the insurance check to be processed? Except for Mama Lena's acute memories of

Big Walter at the moment of receiving the check, the family's grieving for its patriarch seems to be over. Clarity about these issues would enable more accurate interpretations of the impact of Mama Lena's sole influence on her family (e.g., how long she shaped Walter Lee by herself as opposed to raising him with Big Walter) as well as her obvious lack of interest in men.

Hansberry Sought to Undermine the "Mammy" Stereotype

Lisa M. Anderson

Lisa M. Anderson has taught at Purdue University and is an associate professor in the Women and Gender Studies Department at Arizona State University. She is the author of Black Feminism in Contemporary Drama.

In the following selection, Anderson explores the icon of the African American mammy as it relates to Lorraine Hansberry's A Raisin in the Sun. *Though theatergoers were quick to cast Ruth, Beneatha and especially Lena in the role of domineering, emasculating African American women, a careful reading of the play supports the opposite conclusion, Anderson contends. Mama Lena especially, often vilified as an uncaring "mammy" to her son, Walter, instead shows herself to be supportive and nurturing, characteristics that came to be associated with African American women in the mid-twentieth century. In particular, a scene that is often left out of productions of* Raisin *shows Mama in her true role as a matriarch who fosters the well-being of all of her children. Anderson concludes that, while* Raisin *has often been read as reinforcing the Mammy stereotype, Hansberry's intentions were to undermine this demeaning label.*

The icon of the mammy is probably the most recognizable and longest perpetuated image of African American women in American society, and it has been reproduced again and again on stage and screen. If there were any doubt about its pervasiveness, a look at black women presented on many

Lisa M. Anderson, "Mama on the Couch?" in *Mammies No More: The Changing Image of Black Women on Stage and Screen*, Lanham, MD: Rowman & Littlefield, 1997, pp. 9–37. Copyright © 1997 by Rowman & Littlefield Publishers, Inc. All rights reserved. Reproduced by permission.

television sitcoms will reveal her continued presence. The disdain in which African Americans hold this image is nearly as strong; one need only look at *The Colored Museum* (1986). [African American playwright] George C. Wolfe's play includes a mammy, or, as he portrays her, Mama on the Couch, in his satire on African American images in theatre. Wolfe's depiction is associated with the domineering woman who tries to control the lives of those around her, and specifically alludes to Lorraine Hansberry's character Lena Younger from *A Raisin in the Sun* (1959). But whose mammy is she? Is she really Hansberry's Mama? Is there a difference between the origin of mammy and that of Mama Younger? . . .

The Mammy Stereotype

The mammy is descended from a white image of the slave woman, and she first appears in the minstrel show as the "Negro wench"; she is typified visually by the kerchief tied around her head, her apron, and her large size, as well as her racial markers of big lips and a wide nose. This figure is modified and dignified in white-constructed images in later years, but semiotically [in symbolic terms] she remains the same. Her position is still defined by her race; any upward mobility is restricted by her skin color. Like the black men presented in the minstrel show, the original "Negro wench" is an ignorant slave whose speech is filled with malapropisms [incorrect usage and grammar].

The mammy is also the symbol of black motherhood as perceived by whites. In the mythic construction, the black woman "mammy" is the caretaker of the whites' homes and children first, and her own second. Her primary duties are to the whites for whom she works. She must sacrifice the needs of her own family for those of the white family that employs her. Usually she is not shown to have a family of her own at all. The picture of her existing without a family of her own accentuates her status as property, as the children of a slave would have been the master's property. [American novelist] Toni Morrison's description of the characterization of Jim (in [Mark Twain's novel] *Huck Finn*) can be extended to describe this icon of black women—mammies—in the white imagination: "[there is an] apparently limitless store of love and compassion the black [woman] has for [her] white friend and white masters; and [her] assumption that the whites are indeed what they say they are, superior and adult." In essence, then, the mammy is a black woman who focuses her time, love, devotion, and attention on whites, particularly her "adopted" white family, rather than on her own black family.

There were, of course, historical black women who worked as domestics. This work enabled them to help feed their families and supplement or replace the incomes of their husbands, who might not have been able to find work or were only able to find occasional work. The mammy's work was rooted in historical fact, even if other elements of the icon are a departure from historical reality. As [Hansberry's biographer] Margaret Wilkerson states, she was the "neutered, domineering mammy who ruled the roost." Part of the slave woman's labor had been reproduction, but rather than reproducing human beings for their own sake, she produced them as capital for her master. Like the animals owned by the master, she was partnered with the male most likely to produce the most valuable offspring. The black woman's procreation duties were divorced from sexual pleasure.

As a fictional mammy for white children, she is not an authentic mother; in other words, her "mothering" is not connected to the biological process of giving birth. Thus the mammy's sexuality is separate from her motherhood, and the children for whom she cares are not her own. Her position is devoid of the power that would be hers if she were the biological mother of the children for whom she cares. . . .

Mother figures became increasingly important during the early days of the civil rights movement. [Author Paula J.] Giddings states that "it was Black women who represented both moral and social authority when controversial decisions had to be made." The church women of the South provided much needed guidance and support to those who were active. "These women were often looked up to by the whole community because of their wisdom, tenacity, strength, and ability to transcend the oppressive nature of their lives. Wherever the SNCC [Student Nonviolent Coordinating Committee] volunteers stationed themselves in the rural South, such women were invaluable allies." As had been their role for centuries, black women functioned as nurturers of the community as well as of their immediate families. They housed the black student protesters of the SNCC, mothering them in the absence of their own mothers. In the 1950s, [African American gospel singer] Mahalia Jackson commented:

> I believe that right now down South behind most of those brave colored school children and college students you'll find there is still a Negro mother telling them to hold their heads up ... I hear people talking about the Communists being behind the colored students ... it's Negro mothers who believe it's time for their children to fight for their rights and a good education.

An Inappropriate Focus on Walter

By the late 1950s, the strength of black women as nurturers of the race had been recognized in the community, due to the early efforts of club women and educators. It is from this tradition of motherhood that Lorraine Hansberry drew for her first play, *A Raisin in the Sun*. While there has been much criticism of Hansberry's play as integrationist (rather than revolutionary), and while Mama often was and sometimes still is seen as the embodiment of the mammy type who rules the roost, it is evident that Lena Younger is a 1959 reality-based example of the nurturing, protecting, and fighting black woman.

In the original Broadway production and the filmed version, much of the focus of the play was pulled away from the women of the play, and focused instead on Walter Younger and his dreams. When the center of the play is shifted to Walter, his goals and dreams become the most important, and Mama, Beneatha, and Ruth then become the embodiment of the infamous matriarchs . . . , domineering and oppressive to the men of the house. Their caution, dreams, and efforts pale against the patriarchal figure who, in an adoption of the white capitalist model, is meant to make the decisions of the house and to rule his women. In Walter's view, the success of the family depends on him, and it is measured by his financial success and becoming his own boss, even and especially if he makes money at the expense of his own people. Because Walter's dream copies that of the white American dream, the play can be interpreted as a "universal" American story. The emphasis is thus pulled away from race, and white audiences feel that they can see a flattering imitation of themselves in the characters.

Wanting a Better Life

The women of this play, when examined, clearly do not embody [senator and social reformer Daniel Patrick] Moynihan's matriarch [i.e. the domineering, emasculating mammy]. Tim Bond's thirty-fifth anniversary production of the play at the Seattle Group Theatre in September 1994 balances the focus of the play, restoring much of its feminist and revolutionary flavor. Lena is proud of her family, but discouraged by the limited opportunities available to them. She encourages Beneatha to go to medical school and become a doctor, because it is an opportunity for her daughter to "climb." She wishes for a better life for Ruth, Walter, and Travis; the small apartment they all share was never meant to be a home to all of them. In leading her children out of the ghetto, her goal is not integration with whites. Lena says, "Son—I just tried to find

Novella Nelson, as powerful yet maternal Lena, defies the stereotype of the African American "mammy" in this 2005 theatre production of A Raisin in the Sun, *directed by David Lan.* © Donald Cooper/Photostage.

the nicest place for the least amount of money for my family." Walter does not feel this way; instead, he regards her use of the money to buy a house as a betrayal. There will not be enough money for him to invest in the liquor store, and another dream is deferred.

As Lena explains, she feels that it is morally wrong to make money by selling alcohol to their depressed community. Her action is calculated to support the black community, whereas Walter's, scheme emphasizes the dominant capitalist credo in which a man's making money and financial success are the most important goals. Lena is acutely aware of the difficulties faced by black men in American society, particularly Walter's sense of emasculation because of his limited circumstances. This is also a place for Hansberry to critique capitalism; there cannot be "success" for Walter in the classic American sense, i.e., financial success at the expense of someone else. Lena, from her position as a black woman, lacks the power necessary to completely heal his emotional pain. Ruth is also wary of Walter's potential business partners, and for good reason; the money that he invests is stolen by one of his business associates. Like Lena, Ruth wants to help Walter out of his desolation, but she too is unable to give him what he needs. Walter must find for himself the importance of freedom, family, dignity, and community in order to achieve true manhood.

The money that comes into the family does technically belong to Lena, as it is insurance money from her husband's death. She could have used all of the money on herself, as Ruth suggests early in the play, but she chooses to give part of it to her children to help make their lives easier. In this, she embodies the self-sacrificing mother figure. In the Seattle Group Theatre production, the actress playing Lena physically demonstrated the toll that the years have taken on her. Her physical actions were slow, and had a quality of tiredness. She did not stoop her shoulders, but there was a palpable sense of a great weight on her. Lena's dreams are the ones that have been deferred, after all; without the insurance money, they would have "dr[ied] up like a raisin in the sun." Lena tells Ruth of her arrival in their small apartment, with the intention of staying for less than a year—a year that turned into decades. Her dreams of living in a house that she and Big Walter owned were never to come to fruition. With the insurance check, Lena finally has the opportunity to achieve some of her own dreams: to live in a comfortable home, to provide Beneatha money for medical school, to help Walter establish himself and assume his manhood in a positive way. . . .

Lena Is an Understanding Matriarch

Lena is not a stranger to struggle. "Once upon a time," says Lena, "freedom used to be life—now it's money." The values of her generation were focused elsewhere; while they were to a degree on the community, they were also invested in escaping the conditions of the South. In Lena's value system, which follows the traditional value system of black women and Hansberry's own Marxist values, dignity, and family are the most important parts of life; money is important only for its ability to maintain both dignity and family. These values influence Lena's decision to buy the house in Clybourne Park, despite the opposition she knows she will encounter from the whites who live there. . . .

Lena understands the sacrifices that her son has had to make in a world that will not allow him his dreams. Walter is blind to his mother's understanding; he is unable to see beyond his immediate desire for money, thinking that it will gain him the power and respect he desires. He takes his anger out on the women around him; in a conversation with his son, he voices his desire to step into the position of the white patriarch.

In a scene that was not in either the Broadway production or the film version, Ruth and Lena discuss with their neighbor, Mrs. Johnson, the peril into which they are moving. Mrs. Johnson brings in a paper with news of a family that was bombed out of their house in a white neighborhood. The conversation moves on to Lena's children; when Mrs. Johnson claims that there's "nothing wrong with being a chauffeur," Lena counters with

> There's plenty wrong with it. . . . My husband always said being any kind of a servant wasn't a fit thing for a man to have to be. He always said a man's hands was made to make things, or to turn the earth with—not to drive nobody's car for 'em—or—carry they slop jars. And my boy is just like him—he wasn't meant to wait on nobody.

The Seattle production could not include this scene; the financial situation of the theatre could not allow for the hiring of another actress to play Mrs. Johnson. However, because of the efforts of the director and actress, the sentiment of this speech is embodied by Lena in her interactions with Walter. She is critical of her son's acquiescence to the white capitalist patriarchal system, which she views as disruptive and destructive to her family. Walter has assumed that his mother was just trying to run his life and that she didn't understand what his struggles were as a black man, but she had a better grasp of the situation than he himself did. The omission of this scene in other productions and in the film weakens Lena's character; when she is unable to voice her political and economic consciousness, she becomes more interpretable as a stereotypical mammy. Instead of the strength of the history of black women activists behind her, Lena appears conservative and complicitous with white supremacy.

Rejecting the Mammy Stereotype

Lena has spent her life expecting more; she does not intend to take the money offered by the people of Clybourne Park. None of her actions are calculated to please whites, nor is she satisfied with substandard housing or employment. The role has great potential for critiquing the American capitalist system and the detrimental effects it has on African Americans. There is also room for the presentation of the role of Lena Younger as a counterimage of the Moynihan/white imaginary icon of the mammy/matriarch. It is a stark contrast to Annie in [the film] *Imitation of Life* (1959); Lena would never tell her children that they must keep to their places.

In George C. Wolfe's *The Colored Museum*, we can see the mythology of the mammy at work. Wolfe's Mama admonishes her son, when he returns from a hard day dealing with "The Man," to "wipe your feet," drawing directly on Ruth's comments for Walter to "eat your eggs" when he makes a similar complaint. Domineering Mama ignores the struggles of black men. Wolfe also seats Mama, "well-worn," on a couch, reading an oversized Bible. Hansberry's Ruth reappears as a parody of one of the characters in [African American playwright] Ntozake Shange's *for colored girls who have considered suicide/ when the rainbow is enuf*, the Lady in Plaid (1977). Of course, the Lady in Plaid's final line for this segment of the scene is "Not my babies. He dropped them," a direct reference to Shange's Lady in Red mourning her husband's dropping her children from the fifth storey window. The point of the segment comes with Son's speech:

> Wait one damn minute! This is my play. It's about me and the Man. It ain't got nuthin' to do with no ancient temples on the Nile and it ain't got nuthin' to do with Hestia's [goddess of the hearth/household] bosom. And it ain't got nuthin' to do with you slappin' me across no room. It's about me. Me and my pain! My pain!

As Wolfe's creation shows, Hansberry's play has been interpreted in such a way that it serves to reinforce the mammy icon, rather than disperse it, as was Hansberry's intent.

Black Matriarchs
Should Be Admired

Mary Louise Anderson

Mary Louise Anderson taught in Indianapolis, Indiana, and is the author of works on black literature.

In this article, Anderson defines the characteristics of the black matriarch, then shows how these traits are manifested in female characters of three playwrights, Lorraine Hansberry, Langston Hughes, and Alice Childress. Both Mama and Ruth in A Raisin in the Sun *have traits that are stereotypical of black matriarchy, but these are signs of strength that enable such women to persevere through difficult times, according to Anderson. She asserts that the same is true of the matriarchs in dramas by Harlem Renaissance writer Langston Hughes and playwright Alice Childress. Society has forced the black woman into the matriarchal role, Anderson concludes, and the depictions in these plays move audiences toward developing a greater understanding and compassion for such women.*

[F]rench feminist] novelist Simone de Beauvoir once commented, "One is not born a woman. One becomes it by an ensemble of civilization." The "ensemble of civilization" acculturating the American Black woman has had dramatic effects on her role today. She is both condemned and praised by sociologists and psychologists for creating and perpetuating a matriarchal stereotype. In tracing the historical roots of the matriarchal stereotype and in reading some of the social and psychological comments on matriarchy's effects, it is evident that there are common tendencies of matriarchy which can provide a definition. The Black matriarch

Mary Louise Anderson, "Black Matriarchy: Portrayals of Women in Three Plays," *Negro American Literature Forum*, vol. 10, no. 3, Autumn 1976, pp. 93–95. Reproduced by permission.

1. regards the Black male as undependable and is frequently responsible for his emasculation,

2. is often very religious,

3. regards mothering as one of the most important things in her life,

4. attempts to shield her children from and to prepare them to accept the prejudices of the white world.

This matriarchal stereotype is presented clearly in three plays written by famous Black playwrights. By focusing on the matriarchal stereotypes in *Raisin in the Sun, The Amen Corner*, and *Wine in the Wilderness*, one can gain a deeper insight into the problems and controversy of this stereotype.

Matriarchs in *A Raisin in the Sun*

Lorraine Hansberry once commented that *Raisin in the Sun* is not a "Negro play" but rather a play "about honest-to-God, believable, many-sided people who happen to be Negroes." Nevertheless, it is a play about matriarchy. Mama, Mrs. Lena Younger, is a matriarch, and Ruth, her daughter-in-law, struggles with the matriarch role.

The Younger family faces a daily struggle on the southside of Chicago. Into their bleak existence come the hopes and dreams brought by the money Mama is to receive from her dead husband's insurance. Every family member has plans for the money. Although Mama would like to spend it for a new house, she realizes that by ignoring her son Walter's plea for money to invest in a liquor store venture, she has "butchered up his dreams" and has contributed to his emasculation. She considers Walter and the liquor store venture undependable, but she sets aside her doubts and explains to him:

> Listen to me, now. I say I been wrong, son. That I been doing to you what the rest of the world has been doing to you. Walter—what you ain't never understood is that I ain't got nothing, don't own nothing, ain't never really wanted noth-

ing that wasn't for you. There ain't nothing as precious to me ... there ain't nothing worth holding on to, money, dreams, nothing else—if it means it's going to destroy my boy.

And she gives him the money to look after and encourages him to decide about it and to become the head of the family as he should be.

Although Ruth is not the matriarch of the family, in her relationship with Walter one can see the first trait of the matriarch. She sides often with Mama and shares Mama's basic distrust of Walter's plans and doubts his judgment. Like Mama, she is emasculating Walter and is keeping him from asserting himself as protector of the family. At the beginning of the play, when Walter wants to discuss his dreams with her, she answers him with, "Eat your eggs, they gonna be cold." She mothers him instead of listening to and responding to his needs.

Mama exhibits the second trait of the matriarchal stereotype. Religion is an integral part of her life. She wants her children to incorporate her religious ideals into their lives. This wish is most evident when she slaps Beneatha for saying there is no God and makes her repeat, "In my mother's house there is still God." When Mama is furious at Walter for losing the insurance money and is at a moment of great need, she asks God for strength. Her religion sustains her and gives her the strength to be a matriarch.

Mama possesses the absolute devotion to her family true of the matriarchal stereotype. The most important things in her life are her children. When Ruth suggests that she use the insurance money to take a trip, Mama explains that she could never spend the money on herself, but must spend it on the family. Mama decides that the best way to safeguard her family is to move them to a house where they can escape the tensions that plague them. So she makes a down-payment on a house which is "the nicest place for the least amount of money" and sets a sum aside for her daughter Beneatha's schooling. Mama's dreams, her reasons for existence, are her family. She quotes her late husband to Ruth, "'Seems like God didn't see fit to give the black man nothing but dreams—but He did give us children to make the dreams worthwhile.'" Mama is willing to sacrifice anything for her family. When Mama learns that Ruth is planning to have an abortion because she is so desperate about her and Walter's existence and relationship, Mama can understand Ruth's emotions and explains to Walter, "When the world gets ugly enough—a woman will do anything for her family. *The part that's already living.*"

Mama's plant is an ever-present reminder of her matriarchal qualities. When Mama first appears, she tends her plant, just as she tends and nurtures her children. She even says of the plant, "It expresses me." When she envisions her house, she thinks of a garden, a symbol communicating that the house will be the place where the family can grow and flourish in better conditions. It is fitting that her family would give her gardening tools and a gardening hat, symbolizing the tools she needs to nurture them and help their dreams grow.

Baldwin's *Amen Corner*

The Amen Corner by James Baldwin makes a clear statement about Black matriarchy. The main character is Sister Margaret, pastor of a storefront church in Harlem, and the main conflict centers on the relationship she has with her husband Luke and her son David. Mama and Margaret are both matriarchs who come to a realization that the protection they are giving the men in their families is emasculating these men. Both are able to realize and correct only because of the strong unselfish love they have.

Margaret regards the men in her life as undependable. Luke, her husband who has been gone many years, appears at her home worn out and sick. Margaret's relationship with Luke has been a long fight. She comments to Odessa, "The only thing my mother should have told me is that being a woman ain't nothing but one long fight with men." She loved Luke but his salary and musician's lifestyle made it impossible for him to be the protector she needed. Luke tells her, "You ought to of trusted me, Maggie. If you had trusted me till then, you ought to have trusted me a little further." But she cannot trust Luke.

David, her son, plays the piano in the church. Margaret plans for David to follow her as pastor of the church. But David is trying to find himself and make it as a musician behind his mother's back. When Luke returns, Margaret can no longer keep a hold on David. She has emasculated David by making all his decisions for him and has misrepresented his father, his male model. David learns that all this time Margaret has lied about his father. She has told David that Luke was the no-good musician who abandoned them, when, in reality, it was she who left Luke. Luke's presence and words of advice give David the strength to make the decision to leave.

At the end of the play, Margaret loses her church but gains an understanding of the emasculating effect she has had on her men. She understands that David has gone to become a man on his own. She accepts and confesses her need and love for Luke, only to have him die in her arms. Her comments to Odessa show the insight she has gained. She says that she threw her life away by giving it to the Lord and says, "I'm thinking now—maybe Luke needed it more. Maybe David could of used it better." She is able to understand what she has done to her men.

Like many matriarchs, Margaret clings to religion. She is a fiery evangelist who fought with zeal to gain her place as pastor of her church. Her faith is her security. She explains to Odessa, "I tried to put my treasure in heaven where couldn't nothing get at it and take it away from me and leave me alone." The set stresses the importance of religion in Margaret's life. Stage right is the church; stage left is Sister Margaret's apartment kitchen and tiny bedroom. The divided set represents the divided life that Margaret lives, a life both in the church and in the outside world.

Margaret functions in a stereotyped role when she mothers and protects her son. David is as important to Margaret as her religion. She has used the church and religion to create an environment to shelter him. But, at the end of the play, she realizes that this religious environment is no longer real for David and, since she loves him, she must let him go out into the world on his own.

Childress's *Wine in the Wilderness*

Margaret, like Mama and Ruth, is an example of the matriarchal stereotype. While *The Amen Corner* and *Raisin in the Sun* illustrate how these women cope with their matriarchal qualities, *Wine in the Wilderness*, by Alice Childress, illustrates how a Black man learns to cope with the matriarchal stereotype.

The setting of the play is a Harlem tenement during the summer riots of 1964. Working amidst the violence is a Black artist, Bill Jameson, who is attempting to paint a triptych—three paintings that create one work. The triptych, when finished, will express his thoughts on Black womanhood. The first canvas—of an innocent, charming, young Black girl in Sunday dress and hair ribbons—is complete. The second canvas, also complete, is a portrait of his "Wine in the Wilderness"—his ideal of Black beauty. She has a deep mahogany complexion and wears colorful African clothes and a golden headdress. He calls her, "Mother Africa, regal, black womanhood in her noblest form." The third canvas is blank, but he has the unfinished portrait planned. He describes the third woman,

> She's gonna be the kinda chick that is grass roots. No, not grass roots. I mean she's underneath the grass roots. The lost woman, what the society has made out of our women. She's as far from my African queen as a woman can get and

still be female, she's as close to the bottom as you can get without crackin' up. She's ignorant, unfeminine, coarse, rude, vulgar. A poor, dumb chick that's had her behind kicked until it's numb.

Bill and his close friends pride themselves on being up-to-date Afro-Americans who wear natural hairstyles, study Black history, and scorn the Black matriarch and blame her for the emasculation of the Black male. When Bill's friends bring Tommy to him as the model for his third canvas, he finds he must confront the Black matriarch as a person, not as a stereotype. As he becomes involved with Tommy he realizes how unkind and unfair his feelings about the Black matriarchal stereotype have been. He understands that Tommy, the Black matriarch, should be his "wine in the wilderness" because of the beauty of her strength. He says to her, "When they see you on the wall they's gonna say, 'Hey don't she look like somebody we know.'" Bill has learned to see beauty in the stereotype.

Black Matriarchs Deserve Admiration

Bill's realization of the beauty of the Black matriarch is long past due. Women like Tommy, Margaret, Mama, and Ruth deserve admiration. Black matriarchs deserve admiration. White society has forced the Black woman into a matriarchal role. Despite all the problems white society has given her, she has survived and protected her family the best way she can. The Black matriarch should be admired, not condemned, for her strength. By examining matriarchs such as Tommy, Margaret, Mama, and Ruth and the qualities of the matriarchal stereotype that they possess, perhaps we can reach a greater understanding and compassion for the love that motivates the Black matriarch and nourishes her great strength.

Social Issues in Literature

CHAPTER 3

Contemporary Perspectives on Gender

Feminism Has Not Made Women Unhappy

Barbara Ehrenreich

Barbara Ehrenreich is a feminist, essayist, Social Democrat, activist, and the best-selling author of nearly twenty books, including Nickel and Dimed, Bait and Switch, *and* Bright-Sided.

Given a study suggesting that women have become discontented even as they enjoy the fruits of the feminist revolution, noted author Ehrenreich takes issue with those who see a direct correlation between feminism and unhappiness. Ehrenreich suggests that the study's results do not imply that feminism makes women miserable, because happiness is often fickle and difficult to measure; moreover, the study's findings are not conclusive, she maintains. The real motivation behind the release of the study, Ehrenreich writes, is self-promotion. The researchers wish to sell self-help books, not to provide a definitive analysis of women's quality of life.

Feminism made women miserable. This, anyway, seems to be the most popular takeaway from "The Paradox of Declining Female Happiness," a recent study by Betsey Stevenson and Justin Wolfers, which purports to show that women have become steadily unhappier since 1972. [*New York Times* columnist] Maureen Dowd and [author and columnist] Arianna Huffington greeted the news with somber perplexity, but the more common response has been a triumphant: *I told you so.*

On *Slate*'s DoubleX website, a columnist concluded from the study that "the feminist movement of the 1960s and 1970s gave us a steady stream of women's complaints disguised as

Barbara Ehrenreich, "Spare Me the Despair," *The Progressive*, vol. 73, no. 12, December 2009, pp. 14–16. Copyright © 2009 by The Progressive, Inc. Reproduced by permission of *The Progressive*, 409 East Main Street, Madison, WI 53703, www.progressive.org.

manifestos ... and a brand of female sexual power so promiscuous that it celebrates everything from prostitution to nipple piercing as a feminist act—in other words, whine, womyn, and thongs." Or as [antifeminist author] Phyllis Schlafly put it more soberly: "The feminist movement taught women to see themselves as victims of an oppressive patriarchy in which their true worth will never be recognized and any success is beyond their reach. ... Self-imposed victimhood is not a recipe for happiness."

Measuring Happiness

But it's a little too soon to blame [feminist icon] Gloria Steinem for our dependence on anti-depressants. For all the high-level head-scratching induced by the Stevenson and Wolfers study, hardly anyone has pointed out: 1) that there are some issues with happiness studies in general; 2) that there are some reasons to doubt this study in particular; or 3) that, even if you take this study at face value, it has nothing at all to say about the impact of feminism on anyone's mood.

For starters, happiness is an inherently slippery thing to measure or define. Philosophers have debated what it is for centuries, and even if we were to define it simply as a greater frequency of positive feelings than negative ones, when we ask people if they are happy, we are asking them to arrive at some sort of average over many moods and moments. Maybe I was upset earlier in the day after I opened the bills, but then was cheered up by a call from a friend, so what am I really?

In one well-known psychological experiment, subjects were asked to answer a questionnaire on life satisfaction, but only after they had performed the apparently irrelevant task of photocopying a sheet of paper for the experimenter. For a randomly chosen half of the subjects, a dime had been left for them to find on the copy machine. As two economists summarize the results: "Reported satisfaction with life was raised

Activists Betty Friedan, Bella Abzug, and Gloria Steinem, shown here attending the Democratic National Convention in July 1972, fought for women's rights in the United States. Fred W. McDarrah/Getty Images.

substantially by the discovery of the coin on the copy machine—clearly not an income effect."

As for the particular happiness study under discussion, the red flags start popping up as soon as you look at the data. The raw data on how men and women respond to the survey reveal no discernible trend to the naked eyeball. Only by performing an occult statistical manipulation called "ordered probit estimates" do the authors manage to tease out any trend at all, and it is a tiny one: "Women were 1 percentage point less likely than men to say they were not too happy at the beginning of the sample [1972]; by 2006, women were 1 percentage more likely to report being in this category."

Differences of that magnitude would be stunning if you were measuring, for example, the speed of light under different physical circumstances, but when the subject is as elusive as happiness—well, we are not talking about paradigm-shifting results.

Unclear Data

Furthermore, the idea that women have been sliding toward despair is contradicted by the one objective measure of unhappiness the authors offer: suicide rates. Happiness is, of course, a subjective state, but suicide is a cold, hard fact, and the suicide rate has been the gold standard of misery since sociologist Emile Durkheim wrote the book on it in 1897. As Stevenson and Wolfers report—somewhat sheepishly, we must imagine—"contrary to the subjective well-being trends we document, female suicide rates have been falling, even as male suicide rates have remained roughly constant through most of our sample." Women may get the blues; men are more likely to get a bullet through the temple.

Another distracting little data point that no one, including the authors, seems to have much to say about is that while "women" have been getting marginally sadder, black women have been getting happier and happier. To quote the authors: "Happiness has trended quite strongly upward for both female and male blacks. . . . Indeed, the point estimates suggest that well-being may have risen more strongly for black women than for black men." The study should more accurately be titled "The Paradox of Declining White Female Happiness," only that might have suggested that the problem could be cured with [the dark skin pigment] melanin and [antiwrinkle treatment] Restylane.

But let's assume the study is sound and that (white) women have become less happy relative to men since 1972. Does that mean that feminism ruined their lives?

Not according to Stevenson and Wolfers, who find that "the relative decline in women's well-being . . . holds for both working and stay-at-home mothers, for those married and divorced, for the old and the young, and across the education distribution"—as well as for both mothers and the childless. If feminism were the problem, you might expect divorced women to be less happy than married ones and employed women to be less happy than stay-at-homes. As for having children, the presumed premier source of female fulfillment, they actually make women less happy.

And if the women's movement was such a big downer, you'd expect the saddest women to be those who had some direct exposure to the noxious effects of second wave feminism [from the early 1960s to the late 1970s]. As the authors report, however, "there is no evidence that women who experienced the protests and enthusiasm of the women's movement in the 1970s have seen their happiness gap widen by more than for those women who were just being born during that period."

What this study shows, if anything, is that neither marriage nor children make women happy. (The results are not in yet on nipple piercing.) Nor, for that matter, does there seem to be any problem with "too many choices," "work-life balance," or the "second shift." If you believe Stevenson and Wolfers, women's happiness is supremely indifferent to the actual conditions of their lives, including poverty and racial discrimination. Whatever "happiness" is . . .

Just a Sales Pitch

So why all the sudden fuss about the study, which first leaked out two years ago [in 2007] anyway? Mostly because it's become a launching pad for a new book by the prolific management consultant Marcus Buckingham, best known for *First, Break All the Rules and Now, Discover Your Strengths*. His new book, *Find Your Strongest Life: What the Happiest and Most Successful Women Do Differently*, is a cookie-cutter classic of the positive-thinking self-help genre. He begins with the heart-wrenching quotes from unhappy women identified only by their email names (Countess1, Luveyduvy, etc.), then the stories of "successful" women, followed by the obligatory self-administered test to discover "the role you were bound to play" (Creator, Caretaker, Influencer, etc.), all book-ended with an ad for the many related products you can buy, including a "video introduction" from Buckingham, a "participant's guide" containing "exercises" to get you to happiness, and a handsome set of "Eight Strong Life Plans" to pick from.

It's an old story: If you want to sell something, first find the terrible affliction that it cures. In the 1980s, as silicone implants were taking off, the doctors discovered "micromastia"—the "disease" of small-breastedness. More recently, as big pharma searches furiously for a female Viagra, an amazingly high 43 percent of women have been found to suffer from "Female Sexual Dysfunction," or FSD. Now, it's unhappiness, and the range of potential "cures" is dazzling. Seagram's [liquors], Godiva [chocolates], and Harlequin [romance fiction publishers], take note.

Men Should Support Feminism

Mandy Van Deven

Mandy Van Deven is a writer and blogger who often writes about women's issues. She is associate editor of the website girl future.com, a resource for young girls.

In the following viewpoint, Mandy Van Deven observes that more men are recognizing the inherent inequalities in the way men and women have been treated historically and are confronting issues of sexism. What such men realize is that feminism benefits both sexes. Male feminists should understand, she explains, that their voices are sometimes heard above women's voices by virtue of their privileged position in society. Men must acknowledge this privileging and help to undermine patriarchal dominance, she believes. The rigid standards of masculinity that have promoted male authority are slowly changing as society evolves, and this is helping to encourage a less patriarchal society. Van Deven concludes that sexism, misogyny, and other gender ills will not end until men take responsibility for this work.

During my five years as a community organizer at Girls for Gender Equality in Brooklyn, I was frequently asked to recommend a program for young men that could help them examine gender expectations and male privilege. Without hesitation, I would tell them about Brotherhood/Sister Sol.

When I first met the organization's co-founders Khary Lazarre-White and Jason Warwin in New York, I was impressed with their organization's commitment to feminist principles. Lazarre-White explains why it is important for men to be involved in feminist work:

Mandy Van Deven, "Is Feminism Men's Work, Too?" *Herizons*, vol. 23, no. 2, Fall 2009, pp. 16–21. Copyright © 2009 Herizons Magazine, Inc. Reproduced by permission.

"It is essential for men to take an active role in the work to counteract sexism and misogyny because it is our responsibility. Sexism is not the problem of women—it is the problem of men," he believes. "It is personally important for me to do this work because I try to live my life by a moral and ethical compass, and I know that fighting sexism is a daily lived responsibility—from structural organizational work decisions, to personal relationships, to how one lives one's life."

The Reality of Male Feminism

Brotherhood/Sister Sol is committed to deconstructing sexism and misogyny, promoting sexual education and responsibility and reducing gender bias as part of its youth development model. Further, it aims to empower black and Latino young women and men to develop into critical thinkers and community leaders. These men are probably not the faces that immediately spring to mind when one imagines what a feminist looks like, though perhaps they should be.

Men like Lazarre-White and Warwin may be rare. However, there have always been men who have supported women's greater participation in social and political spheres. With her recent book *Men and Feminism*, Shira Tarrant has penned an introductory tome explaining the relevance of feminism to men's lives. The book documents how men's promotion of women's full citizenship can be found throughout history. Tarrant, a professor at California State University–Long Beach, traces such support back as far as the philosophical work of [Greek philosopher] Plato's *The Republic* and [Egyptian jurist and women's rights advocate] Quasim Amin's *The Liberation of Women*. And while her application of the label "feminist" may be anachronistic, her point that male support of women's subjugation has never been universal is well taken.

And yet the idea of a male feminist as either mythic or oxymoronic [a contradiction in terms] persists today. The reasoning seems to be that since feminism is a struggle about women gaining rights, there is no legitimate role for men in that struggle.

However, Rick Taylor, a professor of English and women's studies at East Carolina University, offers proof that men have an important role to play. He shared his thoughts on why it is too simplistic for men to say they are feminist because they care about women's issues.

"Feminism is an important part of my identity and belief system. It informs my professional life, my home life, my sense of spirituality, and my sense of my own past," he explains. "It's a response to the terrible damage done by gender oppression and continued inequality, and an expression of the urge within towards liberation and freedom of self-expression."

Feminism Also Benefits Men

Feminist theorists such as bell hooks, Alice Jardin, Aaronette M. White and Rubaiyat Hossain have written about the many ways feminism benefits men in addition to women. Those benefits include increased societal acceptance of people who do not conform to rigid gender binaries [dualities], prioritizing fatherhood in the lives of children and decreasing the emotional stress of being the sole or primary financial provider for one's family—which, in turn, can positively affect mental and physical health.

Today, an increasing number of feminist men are speaking for themselves about why and how they support gender equality. One of them is John Savel, an education professional in Ann Arbor, Michigan, who spoke about gender conditioning. "I have serious anxiety issues," he explains, "and I have been wondering if part of that has to do with the pressure I have [to be traditionally masculine] and my failure to act that way."

As Savel demonstrates, feminism makes visible the ways gender expectations shape our experiences and opportunities. In contrast to the notion that feminist men are either "whipped" [dominated by a woman] or else pretending to support women's rights in order to get laid, many men are strong allies in the gender equity movement. Modern-day activists like Martin Dufresne of Montreal Men Against Sexism and anti-porn activist Robert Jensen are furthering a male feminist agenda and using their own experiences and perspectives to convince other men that feminism supports people of all gender identities.

Men's Feminist Groups

Although Montreal Men Against Sexism (1979–2003) is no longer active, during its heyday the group worked to discredit the emerging anti-feminist "men's rights" groups in Quebec. Former director Dufresne says, "I may be an incurable optimist, but I really think patriarchy has become unstable and is in the process of being brought down. I consider myself lucky to live at this time and be part of this process, along with my feminist friends whose political intelligence constantly awes me."

The Coexist Initiative (Kenya), Men for Change (Canada), Samyak (India) and the Men's Resource Centre of Saskatoon [Canada] also work to move feminism forward around the globe. But the challenge of undoing institutionalized male privilege is complicated, and because institutional privilege is largely invisible to those who have it, men must be rigorous in their attempts at self-reflection.

From the White Ribbon Campaign (Canada) to Men Can Stop Rape (U.S.), to Program H (Brazil), anti-violence work is perhaps that most common form of male feminist activism. Perhaps the most off-cited example of male feminism since its inception in 1991, on the second anniversary of The Montreal Massacre, the White Ribbon Campaign has become the largest male-led effort worldwide to educate boys and men about gender violence. In Canada, the organization coordinates an annual national public awareness campaign that begins on the

International Day for the Eradication of Violence Against Women (November 26) and ends twelve days later on Canada's National Day of Remembrance and Action on Violence Against Women (December 6) while supporting locally organized events throughout the year.

Combating Violence Against Women

Physical and sexual violence has prompted many feminist men to lead violence prevention work around the world, particularly with other men. By modelling anti-sexist behaviour, men teach each other to see the ways one's gender is socially constructed and works to shape one's thoughts, actions and sense of entitlement.

Taylor explains: "I would guess that men who grow up in abusive or alcoholic environments tend either to reproduce them as adults or fight against them." For many men, the choice is the latter.

As Australian sociologist Michael Flood writes in "Engaging Men in Ending Men's Violence against Women," including boys and men in feminist advocacy does make a difference. But the task of enacting social change is at times fraught with complications, especially if men's strategies to combat sexism do not involve analyzing and disassembling their own power, empowering women, or both.

For example, anti-violence programs run by men for men can unexpectedly reinforce men's position of social authority and undermine the legitimacy of women's voices by subtly conveying through the structure of the program that violence against women is unacceptable only because another man says it is.

Swedish artist Gabriel Bohm Calles explains: "It's what other men think that counts. And the pressure men live under in their lives mostly comes from other men."

Male Voices Are Privileged

What Calles is saying is that it is possible to shift the dialogue without changing the underlying power dynamic. Therefore, an ideal program model is one co-facilitated by men and women in order to model the type of egalitarian behaviour one wishes to promote.

This dynamic was addressed by Flood, who told delegates at the Australian Women Speak: Inaugural National Women's Conference in 2001 that "responses to men's involvement in gender issues are themselves shaped by patriarchal privilege."

First, Flood noted, men's groups often receive greater media attention and interest compared to similar groups of women. "This is partly the result of the former's novelty," he told the conference, "but it is also a function of the status and cultural legitimacy granted to men's voices in general."

Flood went on to say that "men acting for gender justice receive praise and credit [especially from women] which is often out of proportion to their efforts." In other words, "any positive action by men may be seen as gratifying in the face of other men's apathy about and complicity in sexism." Flood also noted that men are able to draw on institutional privilege to attract levels of support and funding rarely granted to women. "This can of course be turned to strategic advantage," he concluded.

The danger in invoking that privilege, of course, is that it may marginalize women's voices in their own movement, inadvertently reinforcing patriarchal values. Ignoring these issues also prevents male feminists from acknowledging any benefits they receive from institutional sexism. Many women have called men to task for enacting their male privilege, only to hear a defensive denial in response. This isn't necessarily a response specific to men; it is a response that arises in all people with privilege. White anti-racist activists also fail, at times, to recognize their privilege, even when people of colour point out ways in which they hold on to their power.

In her viewpoint Van Deven contends that men must take responsibility to support women's rights. Here an unidentified man protests for women's rights. Barbara Freeman/Getty Images.

Confronting Male Privilege

Possessing privilege means one has the ability to choose not to be aware of that privilege when it isn't convenient. In a time when one feels defensive, the best initial response is to listen, listen and then listen some more.

"The most difficult challenge, and one that I had to confront very early, was the assumption that by privilege of being male I had something interesting to say," offers Ashvin Kini, a graduate student of literature at UC–San Diego and writer for the *Feminist Review* blog. "I needed to learn to shut up, sit back and LISTEN. While I wholeheartedly believe that men should identify as feminist, that means being able to recognize our need to listen and reflect."

Kini concludes, "I may identify as feminist, but I do not always have the right to offer my opinion on feminist issues."

For male feminists, maintaining an awareness of their own privilege in order to vigilantly disassemble male dominance is crucial. It is not enough to talk the talk; one must also incorporate principles of equality into one's daily life. This means not only treating individual women with respect (for example, sharing household and child care responsibilities, encouraging women's financial independence and economic success) and refusing to be complicit when other men demonstrate sexist behaviour, but also taking steps to shift societal dynamics that benefit men as a group (such as raising awareness about the links between dominant constructions of masculinity and gender-based violence, promoting reproductive justice policies and rejecting unearned authority).

Confronting male privilege requires an intersectional analysis of oppression that includes class, race, sexuality, geographic location and gender identity. And it means recognizing that while individual power varies, in most places around the world men receive institutional benefits and power to the detriment of women.

Being accountable for the deconstruction of male privilege means men should find creative ways to undermine and disassemble patriarchy, instead of pulling the rug out from under women. This might take the form of organizations run by men rejecting unearned benefits for their involvement in gender equity work and steering media and potential financial supporters toward like-minded organizations run by women. It can mean men use the remuneration of their privilege to tap into male-dominated resources that are less accessible to women. It means taking steps to build a dialogue and a strategy that support and centralize women's needs, strengths and abilities to make self-determined choices.

Filmmaker Byron Hurt does this in *Beyond Beats and Rhymes*, a documentary that explores "masculinity, sexism, violence and homophobia in today's hip hop culture." Instead of blaming an amorphous "hip hop culture" for women's degradation, Hurt turns the lens to focus squarely on the part men play in creating a limited conception of black masculinity that imprisons both men and women. He does this by featuring interviews with men and women, putting the onus for developing solutions on men.

In March 2009, the Global Symposium on Engaging Men & Boys in Achieving Gender Equality took place in Rio de Janeiro. The first worldwide gathering of its kind, the conference brought together 450 participants from 80 countries and organizations including Brazil's Promundo Institute and Instituto Papai, Canada's White Ribbon Campaign, the United States' Save the Children and several coalition organizations like MenEngage Global Alliance and the United Nations Population Fund (UNFPA). The four-day exploration of men and feminism ended with a declaration that includes a call to action for men and boys to support feminism worldwide.

The declaration states, in part: "We are here because we know that the time when women stood alone in speaking out against discrimination and violence ... is coming to an end. We are gathering not simply to celebrate our first successes, but, with all the strength we possess, to appeal to parents, teachers, and coaches, to the media and businesses, to our governments, NGOs [nongovernmental organizations], religious institutions and the United Nations, to mobilize the political will and economic resources required to increase the scale and impact of work with men and boys to promote gender equality."

Taking Male Feminism to the Next Level

The men who organized the Global Symposium on Engaging Men & Boys in Achieving Gender Equality are taking male feminism to the next level. They are attempting to move beyond smaller, short-term interventions toward long-term, large-scale change. The conference yielded a plan of action for individuals, governments, community-based organizations, media and entertainment professionals, donors and private sector workers to incorporate feminism into their lives and work.

On an individual level, more men are taking classes or majoring in women's studies than ever before. We are beginning to see new models of masculinity in "bromance" films, a sign that men are becoming increasingly aware of themselves as gendered. As more men enter traditionally pink-collar [women's] professions such as nursing and primary school education, rigid standards of masculinity are slowly changing, binary gender roles are challenged and new models of what author Shira Tarrant calls "anti-racist, class-conscious, pro-queer, feminist manhood" are created.

Gender inequality is a historic inheritance that an increasing number of men are disavowing. Men's involvement in the women's rights movement can help create better, more equitable models for future generations of boys and girls. Full social, political and economic equality may still be a long way away, but the movement is more effective working in concert with male feminist allies.

As Lazarre-White puts it, "The issues of gender inequity, of structural sexism, of misogyny and the objectifying of women as commerce and property—these issues will not be deconstructed merely by women talking with girls. Men must take responsibility as well for this work. And we should not be commended for it. It is what evolved, ethical, moral men should be expected to do."

Black Men and Women Should Stop Comparing Their Victimization

Stephanie L. Phillips

Stephanie L. Phillips is professor of law at the State University of New York at Buffalo. She teaches in the areas of conflict of laws, securities regulation, law and religion, and race and American law.

In the following article, Phillips states that Anita Hill's testimony against Supreme Court nominee Clarence Thomas in 1991 confirmed suspicions among black men that black women often prove disloyal. This notorious event, along with a 1994 report by Orlando Patterson, suggested a crisis between black men and women and increased divisiveness over the issue of which gender is more oppressed by the white establishment. Some black feminists, such as bell hooks, responded to Patterson angrily, but others suggested that African Americans must move past the politics of blame and focus on bettering life for all, not merely for women or men. The latter attitude, Phillips believes—citing the feminist writings of novelist Alice Walker (The Color Purple)—is the proper stance. Black feminists need to adopt a humanist perspective and work toward betterment for both sexes.

In 1991, Clarence Thomas was nominated to the Supreme Court of the United States. Because Thomas is a very conservative Republican who opposed affirmative action and was antipathetic to many commonly held views of African Americans, his nomination posed a dilemma for some. On the one

Stephanie L. Phillips, "Beyond Competitive Victimhood: Abandoning Arguments That Black Women or Black Men Are Worse Off," in *Progressive Black Masculinities*, edited by Athena D. Mutua, Lynn, MA: Routledge, 2006, pp. 217–223. Copyright © 2006 by Taylor & Francis Group, LLC. Republished with permission of Taylor & Francis Group, LLC, conveyed through Copyright Clearance Center, Inc.

hand, to have an African American on the court seemed a good thing. On the other hand, this particular African American was unlikely to represent the black community's point of view or to advance its interests. For many, the dilemma intensified when Anita Hill, also a very conservative Republican, testified at Thomas's confirmation hearings. She gave explicit examples of the highly sexualized commentary that regularly poured from Thomas's mouth when he headed the Equal Employment Opportunity Commission, where Hill had worked as his subordinate. According to Hill, Thomas's foul musings created such a hostile environment as to constitute sexual harassment.

Black Women and Loyalty

Although a few applauded Hill's courage and certainly hoped her testimony would derail the Thomas nomination, most African Americans were appalled. The sexual explicitness on national television seemed akin to a pornographic display that reinforced white America's worst stereotypes about oversexed, degenerate black people, particularly black males. Moreover, the fact that a black woman was betraying a black man to whites—the Senate, white feminists, white America at large—meant that, once again, African Americans had to tangle with the hoary issue of whether black women owe unconditional support to any and all black men who stand before the white power structure. This supposed duty of loyalty comes from the idea that black Americans must present a united front against our enemy: white supremacy and its minions. Moreover, and more problematically, the obligation for black women to stand by our men is often assumed as a form of overcompensation: Black women are continually trying to disprove the allegation that we collude with white men to the detriment of black men. Colloquially, this charge is captured in the trope [figure of speech] that "ain't nobody so free as a black woman and a white man." In the aftermath of the Thomas hearings, many scholars ruminated on the long history and seeming intractability of the trope, which implies, among other things, that black men are worse off than black women in the social order structured by American white supremacy. According to [American historian] Nell Painter,

> The Black-woman-as-traitor-to-the-race is at least as old as *David Walker's Appeal* of 1829, and the figure has served as a convenient explanation for racial conflict since that time ... [I]t should be remembered that in the tale of the subversion of the interests of the race, the Black female traitor—as mother to whites or lover of whites—connives with the white man against the Black man. Such themes reappear in *Black Skin, White Masks*, by Frantz Fanon; in *Black Rage*, by William Grier and Price Cobbs; and in *Madheart*, by LeRoi Jones, in which the figure of "the Black woman," as "Mammy" or as "Jezebel," is subject to loyalties to whites that conflict with her allegiance to the Black man. Unable to extricate herself from whites, the Black-woman-as-traitor misconstrues her racial interests and betrays Black men's aspirations to freedom.

In Painter's view, Thomas deliberately cast Hill in the role of black-woman-as-traitor-to-the-race. Indeed, one prominent black commentator explained to the *New York Times* how Hill evoked in black men an age-old fear that black women would betray them. Specifically, Alvin Poussaint, preeminent African American psychiatrist, had this to say about Hill's testimony that Thomas, now associate justice of the Supreme Court, had sexually harassed her: "There's a high level of anger among Black men, be they low-income or professional, that Black women will betray them; that Black women are given preference over them; that white men like to put Black women in between them to use them."

The charge that black women collude with white men— again, colloquially, "ain't nobody so free as a black woman and a white man"—is sexual in origin, but has been generalized to the proposition that black men suffer more than black women as victims of white supremacy. The prime response of black feminists, including critical race theorists, has been to demonstrate that black women's sexuality has made us peculiarly vulnerable to white racist oppression rather than being a source of privilege. Black feminists have also directed a great deal of attention to demonstrating that, in the aggregate, black women are economically more disadvantaged than black men. Another prong of the response by black feminists has been to demonstrate that the false assumptions about black women's motivations and conditions that underlie the "ain't nobody so free" trope are used to excuse black male violence, to privilege black male experience, and to validate black male sexism. Furthermore, black feminists have frequently pointed out that the trope deflects attention from the social institutions and ideologies that are the principal sources of African American oppression and that asking women to disempower themselves to bolster male ego is a formula that helps no one.

Black feminists must continue to expose the myths, misinformation, and lies used to deny the oppression of black women. However, the defense of black women and explication of our suffering can be taken too far, yielding statements by some black feminists implying that black males consistently benefit from gender privilege, not only in relationships with black females but also in the comparative advantages of black males and females in American society at large. Correcting this distortion, which had been discernible in the work of some contemporary black feminists, was a probable precondition for furthering feminist ideas among black women, who live with and observe black men on a daily basis. If black feminism seemed to deny or to misapprehend the realities of black male oppression, then it was unsurprising that black women were reluctant to describe themselves as *feminist*.

Some black feminists had done important work on the question of the gendered oppression of black males, but there was no unanimity on the question whether black feminists should abandon the formulation that black women are more oppressed than black men or on the question whether it is beyond the scope of black feminism to pay particular attention to the forms of racist oppression specifically directed against black men. This lack of consensus caused theoretical and practical difficulties for black feminists, particularly in relation to the broad antiracist movement, tensions amply illustrated by Orlando Patterson's 1994 "Blacklash" article and the black feminist responses to Patterson included in a 1995 symposium.

A Crisis in Relations

According to Patterson, there is a crisis in relations between African American men and African American women, as evidenced by, among other things, a declining marriage rate. The principal factor contributing to the African American gender crisis is that African Americans are racially subordinated and live in a hostile social, political, and economic environment. However, problems also are internally generated or perpetuated within the African American community.

With respect to the lower classes, Patterson traced the violent, misogynistic, and irresponsible behavior of many young African American males to the fact that they have been reared in single-parent households headed by women who are prone to brutal, abusive disciplinary methods. Furthermore, Patterson ventured into Freudian [of psychiatrist Sigmund Freud] theory: Because lower-class, black, male children have neither a father nor an effective father substitute present to model a healthy form of masculinity, they lapse into violence and predatory sexuality as the only means available for overcoming attachment to their mothers. Moving on to examine the gender crisis in middle-class black America, Patterson pointed to a profound ideological misfit between African American women and men: "[R]esearchers have found serious mismatches and contradictions in the attitudes of middle-class black men and women. While middle-class black women have, with one notable exception, the most advanced set of gender attitudes in the nation, black men tend to remain highly traditionalist, believing in male dominance ideology in familial relations." Having laid out his analysis of the gender crisis among lower- and middle-class African Americans, Patterson accused black feminists of having obscured these issues. Specifically, he blamed black feminists for distorting the inquiry into the actual state of African American gender relations by adopting the divisive and inaccurate formulation that African American women are more oppressed than African American men.

As to the comparative situations of African American women and men, Patterson is himself both unclear and self-contradictory. Given the impossibility of making coherent sense of his various propositions, it is not in the least surprising that two prominent black feminist theorists had starkly different responses to Patterson's article.

Feminist Responses

First, there is [African American feminist writer] bell hooks, who responded to Patterson's essay with indignation. Viewing Patterson's essay as "anti-feminist propaganda in Blackface," she pointed out that "[s]exist and misogynist thinking has always blamed mothers for the psychological dilemmas males face." In response to Patterson's assertion that "contemporary African American feminist thought has badly obscured our understanding of gender relations," hooks objected to his "willingness to lump all black women who advocate feminist thinking together, even though our perspectives are not the same." Hooks's anger at the fact that Patterson made sweeping generalizations about feminism was largely justified. Indeed, Patterson appeared totally unaware that the double-burden formulation he found problematic had been the subject of analysis, discussion, and critique by black feminists for at least fifteen years. Patterson wrote, "It has become almost a truism in discussions of black gender relations that African-American women are uniquely oppressed with a double burden. In today's usage, added to the burden of racism is the double jeopardy of mainstream gender discrimination. Following the Thomas hearings, in which an African-American woman was pitted against an African-American man, . . . many commentators and analysts emphasized yet a third burden experienced by African-American women: that of gender prejudice and exploitation by African-American men. . . ."

Patterson, thinking that "the double burden argument, while not strictly incorrect, obscures more than it illuminates," wanted black feminists to abandon any formulation implying that black women are more oppressed than black men. Hooks's angry retort was, in effect, that many black feminists abandoned that formulation long ago, which Patterson would have known if he had taken feminism seriously. The bottom line is that hooks was angry at Patterson for failing to realize that black feminists had been grappling for years with the issues that had just come to Patterson's attention. This is hooks's description of the strand of black feminism to which she adhered and of which Patterson was apparently ignorant:

> Truthfully, revolutionary visionary feminist thinking by Black females and males is one of the few places we can turn for an account of Black gender relations that does not seek to pit Black women and men against one another in an endless, meaningless debate about who has suffered more. This work courageously acknowledges that white supremacist capitalist patriarchy assaults the psyches of Black males and females alike. It is only by constructively articulating the nature of that assault and developing redemptive strategies for resistance and transformation that we can resolve the crisis of Black gender relations.

In another symposium response to Patterson's "Blacklash" essay, prominent black feminist Michele Wallace recognized, like hooks, that Patterson was raising issues black feminists had been engaging for some time. Unlike hooks, however, Wallace decided not to be angry with Patterson but rather welcomed him into the black feminist discussion.

Wallace began her article by writing that Patterson's "'Blacklash' is a wonderful and important piece." Like hooks, but much more gently, Wallace chided Patterson for inaccurate overgeneralization of black feminist thought. She took issue with a passage written by Patterson, where he objects to "the tendency of black feminists, who dominate the discourse, to confine, and confound, the problems of gender—which concerns both males and females in their relations with each other—with those of women's issues, or, when relational problems are considered, to privilege the standpoint of women, on the assumption that they are always the victims of the interaction. Black men have as much at stake. . . ." Wallace responded that she "no longer see[s] Black feminism as the discourse of victimization." Rather, says Wallace, "In contemporary feminist discourse in the circles I frequent, . . . discussions of female gender and its construction rarely fail to take into account that constructions of female gender need to be thought in conjunction with constructions of masculinity."

Pointing to the lack of unanimity among black feminists on basic issues, Wallace opined that "Black feminism today is . . . an odd and frail creature, not quite fish or fowl," wherein "[m]any black women who practice a brand of feminism can't even agree upon calling themselves feminists." Although Wallace did not agree with everything Patterson wrote in his article, she was inclined to be generous, given the disarray of black feminist thought. Her bottom line with regard to Patterson is this: "The point is that he is proceeding in the right direction and that we need to be thinking along these lines."

For purposes of the present inquiry, the important points in the hooks and Wallace articles are that neither one of them defended the formulation that black women are more oppressed than black men; both implicitly conceded that their early work reflected ideas on the relative position of black women and men to which they no longer adhered; and both had come to include black masculinity within the purview of their work. It may nevertheless be the case, however, that the gendered oppression of black men is not a central black feminist concern, because black feminists prioritize exploration of the conditions in which African American women live and advocacy for African American women. Beyond these priorities, the full scope of black feminism becomes unclear. In fact, there has been such enormous contention surrounding the definition of *black feminism* that some thinkers have abandoned the phrase.

Working Toward a Greater Good

[African American novelist] Alice Walker coined the word *womanist* as, among other things, a synonym for the phrase *black feminist* and as a contrast to *feminism* in general. This is Walker's definition, quoted in full because it has been so influential:

> Womanist 1. From womanish. (Opp. of "girlish," i.e., frivolous, irresponsible, not serious.) A Black feminist or feminist of color. From the Black folk expression of mothers to female children, "You acting womanish," i.e., like a woman. Usually referring to outrageous, audacious, courageous or willful behavior. Wanting to know more and in greater depth than is considered "good" for one. Interested in grown-up doings. Acting grown up. Being grown up. Interchangeable with another Black folk expression: "You trying to be grown." Responsible. In charge. Serious.
>
> 2. Also: A woman who loves other women, sexually and/or nonsexually. Appreciates and prefers women's culture, women's emotional flexibility (values tears as natural counter-balance of laughter), and women's strength. Sometimes loves individual men, sexually and/or nonsexually.

Committed to survival and wholeness of entire people, male and female. Not a separatist, except periodically, for health. Traditionally universalist, as in: "Mama, why are we brown, pink, and yellow, and our cousins are white, beige, and black?" Ans.: "Well, you know the colored race is just like a flower garden, with every color flower represented." Traditionally capable, as in: "Mama, I'm walking to Canada and I'm taking you and a bunch of other slaves with me." Reply: "It wouldn't be the first time."

3. Loves music. Loves dance. Loves the moon. Loves the Spirit. Loves love and food and roundness. Loves struggle. Loves the Folk. Loves herself. Regardless.

4. Womanist is to feminist as purple to lavender.

Walker obviously is very woman oriented. At the same time, two of her phrases seem to press through the boundaries of a black feminism defined solely by reference to the interests of black women. According to Walker, a womanist is committed to survival and wholeness of entire people, male and female, and is traditionally universalist. The refusal to limit their scope to the interests of women and the emphasis on universalism have been prominent emphases in the work of other black feminists, beginning in the late nineteenth century and continuing today.

Patricia Hill Collins is a contemporary black feminist who has drawn particular attention to the need for black feminism to be situated within broader humanist discourses and movements. In Collins's view, though black women experience many different forms of oppression that black feminism must address, black feminism has no special competence regarding all forms of oppression:

Despite African-American women's potential power to reveal new insights about the matrix of domination, a Black women's standpoint is only one angle of vision. Thus Black feminist thought represents a partial perspective. The overarching matrix of domination houses multiple groups, each with varying experiences with penalty and privilege that produce corresponding partial perspectives, situated knowledges, and, for clearly identifiable subordinate groups, subjugated knowledges. No one group has a clear angle of vision. No one group possesses the theory or methodology that allows it to discover the absolute "truth" or, worse yet, proclaim its theories and methodologies as the universal norm evaluating other groups' experiences.

Therefore, black feminism should be considered a subdivision of humanism, for "Black women's struggles are part of a wider struggle for human dignity and empowerment." Even though the core agenda of black feminists may not encompass all forms of oppression, none fall outside the humanist commitments of black feminist thought.

The expansive description of black feminism, as committed to furthering the interests of black women; attentive to the race, class, and gender valences of black women's experiences; and part of a universalist quest for the principles and conditions of human flourishing has many and far-reaching implications. It means, among other things, that black feminists are concerned about issues that do not directly affect black women and that black feminists will not always insist that the interests of black women be given priority, when those interests conflict with other important projects. Nor should black feminist attempt to evade these complexities. The humanist stance is necessary to avoid parochialism, to work effectively for social change, and to develop principled bases for coalition.

The African American Beauty Industry Is Still Controlled by White Corporations

Susannah Walker

Susannah Walker is assistant professor at Virginia Wesleyan College.

In the following excerpt, Walker explains that hairstyles and beauty aids became political statements in the twentieth century, as businesses, black and white, jockeyed for position in the battle to win over African American women. Black-owned businesses that catered to black women were a point of pride in the African American community, but white-owned corporate executives, seeing a lucrative market, moved in. Though their products were not always the most effective, Walker asserts, ad campaigns targeting black women often were. With major names such as L'Oreal and Revlon buying out black-owned companies, she states, the future of the African American beauty market remains unclear.

In a 1987 speech at her alma mater, Spelman College, [African-American novelist] Alice Walker told a part of her own hair history. Placing the story in the context of her spiritual and intellectual growth as she reached forty, Walker told her audience that it took considerable contemplation and soul searching before she realized "in my physical self there remained one last barrier to my spiritual liberation, at least in the present phase: my hair." It was, she asserted, her "oppressed hair" that was holding her back. Walker recalled her hair's beleaguered history: "I remembered years of enduring hairdressers—from my mother onward—doing missionary work on my hair. They dominated, suppressed, controlled." After "experimenting" with long braid extensions while allowing her "short, mildly processed (oppressed) hair" to grow out, Walker reveled in letting her hair do what it pleased. "Eventually," she said, "I knew precisely what my hair wanted: it wanted to grow, to be itself, to attract lint, if that was its destiny, but to be left alone by anyone, including me, who did not love it as it was." As a result, Walker concluded, "the ceiling at the top of my brain lifted; once again my mind (and spirit) could get outside myself."

Beauty and Racial Politics

Like so many intellectual and politically active black women since the mid-1960s, Walker connected her hair, particularly her unprocessed hair, to her racial identity and to notions of personal liberation. Walker's individual story illustrates the central ideas about the larger social significance of African American women's hair and beauty ideals. . . . Letting one's hair "be itself," to the extent that it was supposed to represent an expression of liberation from oppressive beauty ideals, was an important rhetorical tool after 1960 for many black people to collectively and individually define ideas about racial freedom. Still, it was not the first time African American women's hair and appearance were made to take on social and political meaning within black communities. Walker's reference to hair straightening as "missionary work" is an apt one, and not only in the negative sense that beauty culturists sought to "control" and "suppress" black women's hair. African American hairdressers in the twentieth century saw themselves as missionaries of sorts. In the 1920s and 1930s, beauty culture was part of a program of racial uplift; it promised to free black women from labor oppression and poverty. From the 1940s through the mid-1960s, hairdressers, in their rhetoric and actions, took up the ideals and objectives of the civil rights movement, maintaining that their profession, and the appearance of African American women, could represent and promote both black economic independence and interracial harmony. In fact, the rise of natural hair as a statement of black pride was only one in a series of examples of how hair was political for black women in the United States in the twentieth century.

It is important to place African American women's beauty culture in its cultural, economic, political, and historical context to understand the social origins and development of beauty standards for black women from the 1920s to the 1970s. The beauty standards sold by the African American beauty industry and promoted by beauticians and entertainers and in the mass media were, of course, heavily influenced by white America, but there was a more complex process at work than simple emulation of white beauty ideals. Much of the time, African American beauty standards were shaped within black society as much as they were formed in reaction to (let alone imposed by) the majority culture. It is important, therefore, to understand the influence of such factors as migration and urbanization, class dynamics, and the rise of mass consumer culture on the history of African American commercial beauty culture and commercialized beauty ideals. In addition, one must pay close attention to the connections between African American beauty culture and black consumerism in general, linking both to twentieth-century racial politics. African American advertising and marketing boosters throughout the period examined here viewed beauty culture as a special kind of business that exemplified both black consumer power and the potential for successful black entrepreneurship. People like [African American entrepreneur] Claude Barnett and [market researcher] David Sullivan called for greater recognition of black consumerism by white advertisers, using beauty culture as proof that African Americans were eager to buy luxury goods and services while also criticizing white companies that entered the business and advertised their products in black publications. This apparently contradictory mix of integrationism and black economic nationalism actually represented a practical response to the economic and social realities that African American business owners and consumers faced both before and during the civil rights era. Barnett, for example, portrayed black consumers as deserving of the same attention white consumers got, but he also argued that segregation in the 1920s and 1930s necessitated advertising directed specifically at African Americans. Decades later, as legal segregation was being dismantled and white advertisers, more than ever before, were recognizing the value of targeting black consumers, African American marketing experts insisted that continuing cultural differences necessitated continuing race-based advertising strategies. Such arguments, for instance, drove advertisers' creation of the "soul" market in the late 1960s and early 1970s. Thus marketing professionals argued both for inclusion of African Americans as consumer citizens and for special treatment of African Americans as a separate market, all the while perceiving a need to protect independent and successful black enterprises and markets, such as black beauty culture, from too much attention from white corporations.

Black Beauty Companies as a Source of Pride

This position is clarified when placed in the context of black activism in other political arenas during the same period, particularly during the civil rights and Black Power eras. In *Up South: Civil Rights and Black Power in Philadelphia*, Matthew Countryman observes that, during the 1940s and 1950s, black politicians embraced the Democratic liberal coalition that endorsed an integrationist stance on race relations, but that liberalism's limited achievement of racial justice in economic and public institutions in Philadelphia prompted increasing numbers of African American activists to align themselves with Black Power goals and ideologies. But this was not, Countryman argues, always a clear-cut division. Many black political leaders in the city developed a political ideology that effectively meshed liberal components, such as demanding fair access to jobs and a voice in municipal policymaking, with nationalist efforts to control the political and economic futures of African American communities. Similarly, in the case of beauty culture, African American marketing experts could push for more attention from white advertisers and, especially after World War II, racial justice for African American consumers, while maintaining that the survival of black-owned businesses was essential to the growth of black communities.

This was all the more important when black-owned businesses, like those in the beauty culture industry, catered exclusively to an African American clientele. In fact, this component provides an additional explanation for why African American business advocates were so protective of beauty culture in particular. For decades, and for many diverse reasons, the beauty product industry and professional beauticians were sources of pride in African American communities. Entrepreneurs like Madam C. J. Walker and Sara Washington were lauded for their financial success, for their philanthropy, and for providing employment to black men and women. Beauticians were often respected community leaders. All of these people engaged in work that celebrated the beauty of black women within a broader American society that denied it. But this economic and cultural independence rested on the precarious ground of African Americans' financial power to sustain it. This situation was certainly not unique in the history of black entrepreneurial and cultural enterprises. Writing about Motown Record Corporation and racial politics in postwar Detroit [in her book *Dancing in the Street*], Suzanne Smith observes that African Americans in the Motor City were proud that this music company and musical style, which had originated in black Detroit, were so successful across racial lines and throughout the world. Still, although Motown's integrationist appeal has endured to this day, the economic prosperity and independence for many black Detroiters that initially came with it was short-lived, primarily because of the interrelated factors of Detroit's deindustrialization, Motown's move to Los Angeles, and the label's subsequent sale to a white media corporation. Smith concludes that "Motown's business history proves how difficult it is for black capitalism to survive in the global economy, let alone thrive enough to be able to address or promote the needs of black America."

White-Owned Companies Enter the Market

This crucial idea is well illustrated by the beauty industry. Beauty culturists and product manufacturers often stressed their expertise in working with black women's specific hair and complexion needs, and they frequently deployed this argument to discredit white businesses that entered the African American beauty business. But enter it they did. In the 1920s and 1930s, white companies dramatically increased their presence in this market just as the Depression made it more difficult for African American beauty product companies to compete. This trend intensified after World War II. Even as black-owned beauty parlors experienced considerable success in the immediate postwar years, black-owned beauty product companies continued to be challenged for market share by white ones. In recent years, white corporations have bought out many surviving African American beauty product companies, retaining the names and product lines in a modern version of white companies' earlier attempts to pass as black-owned. L'Oreal bought Chicago-based Soft Sheen in 1998 and in 2000 purchased Carson, the white-owned creator of the Dark and Lovely line (which had acquired Johnson Products, of Afro Sheen fame, two years before). In 2002, L'Oreal went so far as to move its entire "ethnic personal care division" into the old Johnson Products Company building on the South Side of Chicago. A 2002 report in the *Chicago Tribune* reported that remaining small black companies were struggling to maintain market share, some banking on direct sales to salons rather than fighting for shelf space in chain drugstores. In 2006, the *Village Voice* ran interviews of two prominent African American celebrity makeup artists. Both complained that, though white companies were making a big show of offering products to black women and, in the phrase of an old Madam C. J. Walker ad, of "glorifying our womanhood" by using megastars like [American actor] Halle Barry (for Revlon) as spokespeople, most had yet to effectively tap the market for black women's cosmetics. In many cases these companies still failed, especially in the area of foundations and concealers, to manufacture products that worked. Yet the makeup artists deemed black companies' products too old fashioned, in terms of packaging or shade choices (Fashion Fair was cited as an example), or too difficult to find in major department stores. Even MAC Cosmetics, the upscale company famous for deliberately creating genuinely multiracial makeup colors and product lines, was blasted in the article for marketing foundations that looked wrong on the dark complexions they had supposedly been designed for. "Most companies fall short in all areas," commented makeup artist Sam Fine. "Having worked for virtually every major cosmetic brand, I've realized that satisfying the needs of women of color is not a priority."

An Uncertain Future

Thus the limits of black capitalism that Suzanne Smith identifies also apply to the history of African American beauty culture. Promotional rhetoric always exaggerated the power of black-owned beauty businesses to provide economic independence for African American women and their communities, but they certainly did more on that score than any national (or global) white corporation ever could. As with Motown, independent African American–owned beauty businesses experienced their apex of success in the period after World War II, an era of affluence for black Americans, especially in the urban-industrial North and West. Smith cites Detroit's economic decline as one important reason that Motown left—the company followed the money to Hollywood—and points out that this move helped pave the way for the sale of the label to MCA, a white-owned corporation. Similar economic forces since the late 1960s have contributed to the recent entry of companies like L'Oreal and Revlon to the African American beauty market through buyouts of black-owned companies. This trend, of course, makes it less likely than ever before that the beauty business will be a vehicle for African American economic power, but that particular problem is an old one. As the *Village Voice* article cited above suggests, these recent developments also put into question whether the beauty demands of black women will be met any more satisfactorily in the future than they were in the past. Just as important, they prompt one to wonder just how (and by whom) those beauty demands will be defined and promoted in the years to come.

For Further Discussion

1. Given the control that she wields over the Younger family, do you view "Mama" Lena as a positive or negative influence on the family? (See Harris, Lisa M. Anderson, and Mary Louise Anderson.)

2. Is feminism a prominent theme in *A Raisin in the Sun*? What parts of the play seem to contradict typical feminist concerns? (See Singh, Friedman, Burke, and Carter.)

3. After reading articles by Bigsby, Harrison, and Cook, do you consider Walter to be his own worst enemy, or is he a victim of white society and his mother's oppressive control?

4. A number of critics have observed that *A Raisin in the Sun* is the first realistic portrayal of an African American family and the dynamics of gender roles within the family structure. How realistic does the portrayal seem to be? (See Fabre, Friedman, Burke, and Carter.)

5. Beneatha is universally regarded as having been modeled after Lorraine Hansberry herself. How does Hansberry construct Beneatha as a complex, three-dimensional fictional character? (See Fabre, Burke, Singh, and Carter.)

6. Contemporary critics are beginning to focus more on Hansberry's lesbianism and its influence on the play. Does Hansberry's attack on racism suggest an implicit critique of heterosexist society or does this seem to be an irrelevant concern? (See Gomez and Ocamb.)

For Further Reading

Maya Angelou, *I Know Why the Caged Bird Sings*. New York: Random House, 1969.

Ralph Ellison, *Invisible Man*. New York: Random House, 1952.

Lorraine Hansberry, *Les Blancs: The Collected Last Plays*. New York: Vintage Books, 1994.

———, *The Sign in Sidney Brustein's Window*. New York: Random House, 1965.

———, *To Be Young Gifted and Black*. Englewood Cliffs, NJ: Prentice-Hall, 1969.

Zora Neale Hurston, *Their Eyes Were Watching God*. Urbana: University of Illinois Press, 1965.

LeRoi Jones (Imamu Amiri Baraka), *Dutchman*. New York: Morrow, 1964.

Ntozake Shange, *for colored girls who have considered suicide when the rainbow is enuf*. New York: Macmillan, 1975.

Alice Walker, *The Color Purple*. New York: Harcourt Brace Jovanovich, 1982.

George C. Wolf, *The Colored Museum*. New York: Grove Press, 1988.

Richard Wright, *Black Boy*. New York: Harper & Bros., 1945.

———, *Native Son*. New York: Harper & Bros., 1940.

Bibliography

Books

Robin Bernstein *Cast Out: Queer Lives in Theater.* Triangulations. Ann Arbor: University of Michigan Press, 2006.

C.W.E. Bigsby *Modern American Drama, 1945–1990.* Cambridge: Cambridge University Press, 1992.

Mary F. Brewer *Race, Sex, and Gender in Contemporary Women's Theatre: The Construction of "Woman".* Brighton, UK: Sussex Academic Press, 1999.

Rudolph P. Byrd and Beverly Guy-Sheftall *Traps: African American Men on Gender and Sexuality.* Bloomington: Indiana University Press, 2001.

Steven R. Carter *Hansberry's Drama: Commitment amid Complexity.* Urbana: University of Illinois Press, 1991.

Sue-Ellen Case *Performing Feminisms: Feminist Critical Theory and Theatre.* Baltimore: Johns Hopkins University Press, 1990.

Anne Cheney *Lorraine Hansberry.* Boston: Twayne, 1984.

Helen Krich Chinoy and Linda Walsh Jenkins *Women in American Theatre.* New York: Theatre Communications Group, 2006.

Roberta L. Coles *Race and Family: A Structural Approach*. Thousand Oaks, CA: Sage, 2006.

Yolanda Flores *The Drama of Gender: Feminist Theater by Women of the Americas*. Wor(l)ds of Change, vol. 38. New York: Peter Lang, 2000.

Samuel A. Hay *African American Theatre: An Historical and Critical Analysis*. Cambridge Studies in American Theatre and Drama. Cambridge: Cambridge University Press, 1994.

Errol Hill and James Vernon Hatch *A History of African American Theatre*. Cambridge Studies in American Theatre and Drama. Cambridge: Cambridge University Press, 2003.

Leslie Crawford Hurley *Gender and Realism in Plays and Performances by Women*. New York: Peter Lang, 2003.

Helene Keyssar *Feminist Theatre and Theory*. New Casebooks. New York: St. Martin's Press, 1996.

Karen Louise Laughlin and Catherine Schuler *Theatre and Feminist Aesthetics*. Madison, NJ: Fairleigh Dickinson University Press, 1995.

Toni Lester *Gender Nonconformity, Race, and Sexuality: Charting the Connection*. Madison: University of Wisconsin Press, 2002.

Carol P. Marsh-Lockett, ed.	*Black Women Playwrights: Visions on the American Stage.* New York: Garland, 1999.
Leith Mullings	*On Our Own Terms: Race, Class, and Gender in the Lives of African American Women.* New York: Routledge, 1997.
Elizabeth J. Natalle	*Feminist Theatre: A Study in Persuasion.* Metuchen, NJ: Scarecrow Press, 1985.
Clinton F. Oliver and Stephanie Sills	*Contemporary Black Drama: From "A Raisin in the Sun" to "No Place to Be Somebody."* New York: Scribner, 1971.
Sandi Russell	*Render Me My Song: African American Women Writers from Slavery to the Present.* London: Pandora, 2002.
June Schlueter	*Modern American Drama: The Female Canon.* Madison, NJ: Fairleigh Dickinson University Press, 1990.

Periodicals

| James Baldwin and Lorraine Hansberry | "Sweet Lorraine / Some Notes Kept by the Lady During the Last Months of Her Life," *Esquire,* vol. 72, no. 5, 1969. |
| Anne Chapman | "Race & Gender: When It Comes to Discrimination Cases, Are Black Women Left to Fend for Themselves?" *Black Enterprise,* February 2008. |

Kira Cochrane "Retrosexual, or Just Misogynist?" *New Statesman*, June 9, 2008.

Ebony "From Boys to Men to Fatherhood: Three Dads Highlight the Importance of Being There for Their Children," June 2006.

Ed Guerrero "The Black Man on Our Screens and the Empty Space in Representation," *Callaloo*, vol. 18, no. 2, 1995.

Cheryl Higashida "To Be(Come) Young, Gay, and Black: Lorraine Hansberry's Existentialist Routes to Anticolonialism," *American Quarterly*, vol. 60, no. 4, 2008.

Brittany Hutson "The 'Coming Out' Challenge: African American Lesbian, Gay, Bisexual, and Transgender Professionals Are Trying to Gain More Ground in Corporate America, but Unchecked Discrimination Still Exists," *Black Enterprise*, November 2009.

Diana Adesola Mafe "Black Women on Broadway: The Duality of Lorraine Hansberry's *A Raisin in the Sun* and Ntozake Shange's *for colored girls*," *American Drama*, vol. 15, no. 2, June 2006.

Adrienne Rich "The Problem of Lorraine Hansberry," *Freedomways*, vol. 19, no. 4, 1979.

Geoff Rolls "Boys Will Be Boys," *Psychology Review*, September 2008.

Harriet Rubin   "Sexism," *Conde Nast Portfolio*. April 2008.

Andrew Stephen   "Hating Hillary: The Ugly Truth About American Sexism," *New Statesman*, May 26, 2008.

R. Welch   "Spokesman of the Oppressed? Lorraine Hansberry at Work: The Challenge of Radical Politics in the Postwar Era," *Souls: A Critical Journal of Black Politics, Culture and Society*, vol. 9, no. 4, 2007.

Margaret B. Wilkerson   "The Dark Vision of Lorraine Hansberry: Excerpts from a Literary Biography," *Massachusetts Review*, vol. 28, no. 4, 1987.

Margaret B. Wilkerson   "The Sighted Eyes and Feeling Heart of Lorraine Hansberry," *Black American Literature Forum*, vol. 17, no. 1, 1983.

Internet Sources

Jeff J. Koloze   "'. . .We a People Who Give Children Life': Pedagogic Concerns of the Aborted Abortion in Lorraine Hansberry's *A Raisin in the Sun*," *Lifeissues.net*, n.d. www.lifeissues.net.

Index

CPSIA information can be obtained
at www.ICGtesting.com
Printed in the USA
LVOW03s0613120118
562774LV00008B/156/P